P9-EDZ-514

JOHN XXIII FELLOWSHIP CO-OP. LTD.
P O. BOX 22, ORMOND, 3204, AUST.
Telephone (03) 596 5258, 596 2323

A SUMMARY OF THE SEVEN SACRAMENTS

By
a Team of Daughters of St. Paul

ST. PAUL EDITIONS

NIHIL OBSTAT:
   Rev. Richard V. Lawlor, S.J.
   Censor

IMPRIMATUR:
   ✠Most Rev. Bernard F. Law, D.D.
   Archbishop of Boston

Scripture texts used in this work are taken from the *New American Bible*, copyright © 1970, by the Confraternity of Christian Doctrine, Washington, D.C., and are used by permission of copyright owner. All rights reserved.

Library of Congress Cataloging in Publication Data
Main entry under title:

A Summary of the Seven Sacraments.

   Includes index.
   1. Sacraments—Catholic Church. 2. Catholic Church—Doctrines. I. Daughters of St. Paul.
BX2200.S82   1984   234'.16   84—11378

ISBN 0-8198-6858-2 p.

Copyright © 1984, by the Daughters of St. Paul

Printed in the U.S.A., by the Daughters of St. Paul
50 St. Paul's Ave., Boston, MA 02130

The Daughters of St. Paul are an international congregation of Women Religious serving the Church with the communications media.

CONTENTS

Seven Saving Signs

Signs of Grace and Actions of Christ

What are the sacraments?

The sacraments are sacred signs through which Christ gives us grace.

Of what are the sacraments signs?

The sacraments are signs of sanctifying grace—a sharing in the very life of God—and of particular sacramental graces; for example, the strengthening of faith or spiritual healing. They are also signs of faith: the faith of the Church and the faith of the person receiving them.

What sort of signs are the sacraments?

The sacraments consist of natural symbols—such as water or bread, the laying on of hands or anointing with oil—together with words which, by God's power, bring about the spiritual transformation that the action suggests.

For most of the sacraments the sign can clearly be distinguished into two "parts." The things and/or actions are called "matter" and the words are called "form."

Why does Christ act through visible signs?

We are composed of body and soul, and Christ has chosen to approach us through this nature of ours. In the Old Testament God spoke to the Chosen People through the voices and writings of the prophets. Then

He took on human flesh in order to share our form of existence, teach us more thoroughly, show us how to live, and—by dying for our sins—leave us an unforgettable example of His love for us. Now He continues to come into contact with us through the words and examples of others, through the Sacred Scriptures, and especially through the sacramental signs. In short, He deals with us as human beings.

Are the sacraments truly actions of Christ?

The sacraments are truly actions of Christ, the Priest, who through them gives us the grace that He merited with the Paschal Mystery of His suffering, death and glorification. In so doing, Christ acts through a human minister, who represents Him.

He gave His sacraments to the Church in order to bring His act of redemption into direct contact with our lives. From the earliest times, the Church has administered the sacraments that Christ instituted.

The sacraments are so truly His actions that the minister's degree of unworthiness has no influence on their effect; provided that the minister intends to "do what the Church does," Christ will act. It is our Savior Himself who removes sin, changes bread and wine into His body and blood, etc.

What is grace?

Sanctifying grace is a sharing in the divine life.

Actual graces are particular helps "for the moment"—light for the mind or strength for the will—to aid one in avoiding evil and doing good.

Sacramental grace helps a person to live according to the particular state in life or condition brought about by the sacrament, giving a "claim," so to speak, to the actual graces needed for the fulfillment of the sacrament's special purpose. In Baptism one receives help to be faithful to the baptismal vows; in

Confirmation, help to profess and spread the Faith; in the Holy Eucharist, closer union with Christ and the members of His Mystical Body; in Penance or Reconciliation, help to purify the soul and avoid future sin; in the Anointing, spiritual strength in the face of temptations and bodily weakness; in Orders, help to exercise well the powers of the ministry; in Matrimony, help to be a loving and faithful spouse, a loving and devoted parent.

It can be seen, therefore, that the sacraments enable us to undertake certain *responsibilities* toward God, self and others. Each sacrament calls for a personal *commitment* on our part.

Does Christ give grace only through the sacraments?

Christ freely gives sanctifying grace, the gifts and the infused virtues to whomever He chooses, including the non-baptized. Always, of course, the proper dispositions must be present.

He also offers actual graces to all—Christians and non-Christians.

However, it is to be expected that *much more* divine life and help will be given to those who encounter Christ in the sacraments, especially if these persons receive the Eucharist frequently and make regular use of the Sacrament of Reconciliation.

Do the sacraments have further effects than those already mentioned?

The Sacraments of Baptism, Confirmation and Holy Orders configure Christians to the priesthood of Christ through a spiritual imprint called a "seal" or "character." Someone who has received one or more of these sacraments has particular rights, duties and powers with regard to worship (as will be explained under each sacrament further on).

The Sacrament of Matrimony establishes a lifelong bond between husband and wife.

The Sacrament of the Anointing of the Sick brings about the consecration of a state of illness.

The Sacrament of the Eucharist is the Real Presence of Jesus Christ in His humanity and divinity.

Each of the above-mentioned effects has a certain permanence about it. For this reason: the sacraments that imprint a character may be received only once; Matrimony may not be received a second time while one's first spouse is living; a sick person may not be anointed twice during the same illness, unless a more serious crisis has developed.

These real effects are sometimes called "reality signs." Although invisible, they are considered as signs of grace—the common reality of all the sacraments.

Our Own Dispositions

Do the sacraments give grace "automatically"?

The sacraments—as instruments of Christ—unfailingly give grace to persons who place no obstacle to its reception, provided that the minister has the intention of "doing what the Church does." The *abundance* of grace received, however, depends on the dispositions of the person receiving the sacrament.

What dispositions are necessary for the reception of a sacrament?

Anyone who has the use of reason must intend to receive the sacrament. (For young children, the *Church's* intention suffices; for the unconscious, a previous unretracted intention is sufficient.)

In the reception of Penance and for the fruitful reception of Baptism some faith and sorrow for sin are necessary; for the fruitful reception of the other sacraments, the state of grace is required—or, phrased negatively, the absence of mortal sin.

Because Baptism and Penance can be received by those who are spiritually dead through sin, these sacraments may be called sacraments of the dead. The other sacraments, which produce their full effect only when the recipient is in the state of grace, are called sacraments of the living.

To receive a sacrament without the required dispositions is to commit a serious sin called sacrilege.

What should a person do if he or she has received a sacrament sacrilegiously?

One who has received a sacrament sacrilegiously must make a good confession (or, if confession is not *immediately* possible, an act of perfect contrition—sorrow for having offended our good and loving Father —with the intention of going to confession soon). All mortal sins are to be confessed, including the sacrilege.

Baptism, Confirmation, Orders, Matrimony and the Anointing of the Sick are *validly* (truly) received if the intention of receiving them is present.* In other words, even in a sacrilegious reception, the sacramental character is imprinted or a state of marriage or of consecrated illness is established. With the removal of the obstacle to grace (through a good confession or perfect contrition), the sacrament also becomes fruitful; that is, grace is received. (Therefore, the *valid* —that is, true—reception of a sacrament is not always the same as its *fruitful*—that is, lawful or worthy—reception.)

Because one can never be sure that his sorrow is perfect, a baptized person who has lost the state of grace must go to confession before receiving the Eucharist, Confirmation, Orders, Matrimony, or—normally—the Anointing of the Sick.

---

*For valid Baptism, as already noted, a certain degree of faith and of sorrow is also necessary.

Initiation—Healing—Vocation

Why are there several sacraments?

There are several sacraments—seven, to be exact —because we have various needs on the spiritual plane, just as we have various physical necessities.

Three sacraments—Baptism, Confirmation and Eucharist—bring about our spiritual birth and growth. These are the sacraments of initiation. All three of them so complement one another that all three are required for full Christian initiation.

Two sacraments—Reconciliation (Penance) and the Anointing of the Sick—bring about spiritual healing. These are the sacraments of healing.

Two other sacraments—Orders and Matrimony —consecrate Christians for the upbuilding of the Church. These are the sacraments of vocation.

The Sacraments and the Church

How are the sacraments related to the Church?

The sacraments have a close relationship to the Church, for she is their guardian and distributor. The minister of a sacrament is a sign of Christ and a sign of the Church. The sacraments manifest the Church and build it up, through the life of grace which they increase in individuals.

The Church herself is sometimes called a great sacrament, for she is a sign of Christ's presence and activity in the world.

Vatican II on the Sacraments

"The purpose of the sacraments is to sanctify men, to build up the Body of Christ, and finally, to give worship to God; because they are signs they also instruct. They not only presuppose faith, but by words and objects they also nourish, strengthen, and express it; that is why they are called 'sacraments of faith.' They do indeed impart grace, but in addition, the very act of celebrating them most effectively disposes the faithful to receive this grace in a fruitful manner, to worship God duly, and to practice charity....

"For well-disposed members of the faithful, the liturgy of the sacraments and sacramentals sanctifies almost every event in their lives; they are given access to the stream of divine grace which flows from the paschal mystery of the passion, death, and resurrection of Christ, the font from which all sacraments and sacramentals draw their power. There is hardly any proper use of material things which cannot thus be directed toward the sanctification of men and praise of God" (Constitution on the Sacred Liturgy, nos. 59, 61).

Baptism

The Sacrament and Its Origin

What is Baptism?

Baptism is the sacrament which sets us free from original (and personal) sin and gives us new life—a participation in the very life of God. By Baptism we are consecrated to the Blessed Trinity, linked to Jesus in the paschal mystery (His death, resurrection and ascension) and made members of Christ's Body, the Church.

What arguments from Scripture do we have regarding the institution of Baptism?

We have clear references to the institution of Baptism from the words of Christ Himself. To the fervent Jewish Pharisee, Nicodemus, Jesus said:

> "I solemnly assure you,
> no one can enter into God's kingdom
> without being begotten of water and Spirit" (John 3:5).

To His earliest followers, the Apostles, Christ gave this mandate:

> "Full authority has been given to me
> both in heaven and on earth;
> go, therefore, and make disciples of all the nations.
> Baptize them in the name
> 'of the Father,
> and of the Son,
> and of the Holy Spirit'" (Matthew 28:18-19).

After the ascension, was Christ's mandate to baptize fulfilled in the early Church?

The Apostles fulfilled this mandate faithfully, as we see from the Acts of the Apostles. For example, in Peter's first discourse he proclaimed:

> "You must reform and be baptized, each one of you, in the name of Jesus Christ, that your sins may be forgiven; then you will receive the Holy Spirit" (Acts 2:38).

Philip, the deacon, in his zeal to proclaim the message of salvation, explained to an Ethiopian court official the words of the prophet Isaiah. As a result the eunuch said, "Look, there is some water right there. What is to keep me from being baptized?" At that request, "Philip went down into the water with the eunuch and baptized him" (Acts 8:37, 38).

The Acts of the Apostles contains several more examples similar to these.

Infant Baptism

Is it right to baptize infants, even though they are not capable of renouncing Satan and making an act of faith?

In the *Credo of the People of God* we read: "Baptism should be administered even to little children who have not yet been able to be guilty of any personal sin, in order that, though born deprived of supernatural grace, they may be reborn 'of water and the Holy Spirit' to the divine life in Christ Jesus."

The wonderful effects of Baptism are the same for infants as they are for adults. When parents (and sponsors) have the intention of encouraging the child to reject sin and live according to faith, there is no good reason for denying the infant the benefits of Baptism. In defense of this teaching, the early Christians often quoted the words of Christ: "Let the children come to me. Do not hinder them" (Matthew 19:14).

Is there a danger in putting off the Baptism of infants for a long period of time?

Children should be baptized within the first weeks after birth. Baptism is necessary for salvation, as we know from the words of Jesus (John 3:5). Therefore the lengthy postponement of Baptism would be dangerous.

What happens to infants who die without Baptism?

Since infants who die without Baptism have committed no sins, many have held that they will live in a place of natural happiness called "Limbo," where, however, they do not see God. Some modern scholars suggest that God will grant these infants the possibility of baptism of desire before death. The Church has made no official declaration on the matter.

Parents and Godparents

What are the duties of a baptized infant's parents?

Parents must see to it that their children are brought up according to the teachings of Christ and the Church. Failure to perform this duty is a serious matter, since God has entrusted the spiritual as well as the natural care of the children to them first of all.

What are the duties of the sponsor or godparent toward the baptized infant?

The sponsor must be a good-living Catholic, generally no younger than sixteen, who has received both Confirmation and the Holy Eucharist. It is suggested that anyone intending to become a godparent should review his practice of the Faith and prepare himself to accept this obligation with a right intention. Godparents must see to it that their godchildren are raised as good Catholics if this is not done by the parents.

Can an adult be admitted to Baptism without a godparent?

An adult should not be admitted to Baptism without a godparent. This is a very ancient custom in the Catholic Church. The godparent helps the person prepare well for Baptism and afterward aids him to persevere in the Faith and in his life as a Christian.

May a non-Catholic act as a godparent?

If the non-Catholic is a baptized and believing Christian from a separated Church he (she) may act as a Christian witness, if this is requested by the parents, along with a Catholic godparent. (The norms for various ecumenical cases should be followed.)

What does a godparent do at the Baptism?

A godparent testifies to the faith of the one to be baptized, or in the case of an infant he, together with the child's parents, professes the faith of the Church.

What should parents keep in mind when naming their children?

Parents should avoid giving a name that is foreign to a Christian mentality.

The Minister of Baptism

Who may administer the Sacrament of Baptism?

The bishop, priest or deacon is the usual minister of Baptism, but in the danger of imminent death anyone *may* and sometimes *should* baptize. No one, however, may baptize himself.

Does the "extraordinary" minister of Baptism have to be Catholic?

No, the extraordinary minister can be anyone— man, woman or child, Catholic or non-Catholic, atheist or pagan—as long as he or she administers the sacrament correctly and does it with the intention of "doing what the Church does."

How is Baptism given in an emergency?

When cases of emergency arise, private Baptism consists of simply pouring plain water over the forehead of the person being baptized, while saying, "I baptize you in the name of the Father and of the Son and of the Holy Spirit." (When necessary, the water may be poured on another part of the body instead of on the forehead.)

Unless an infant is in danger of death, he should not be baptized without the permission of a parent or guardian. But if there is danger of death, even the child of non-Catholic parents can lawfully be baptized, even against the parents' will.

An adult who is in danger of death can be baptized if he has some knowledge of the principal truths of faith, has in any way manifested an intention of receiving Baptism, and promises to keep the requirements of the Christian religion.

Is lay Baptism as valid as that administered by the priest?

Yes. When properly given, lay Baptism is as valid as Baptism given by a priest.

However, if the baptized person recovers, a Church ceremony should be held so that the other rites associated with Baptism may be performed.

The "Sign" of Baptism

What is the sacramental sign of Baptism?

The water and the words make up the sign of Baptism.

What is their significance?

The water is a sign that sin is being destroyed, and the life of grace is being given. The words represent the beginning of a new and lasting relationship with the Blessed Trinity.

Is there a special kind of water used for Baptisms?

For solemn Baptisms the minister uses baptismal water, which is natural water blessed with special prayers.

In cases of necessity any natural water may be used, such as, for example: seawater, rainwater or even mineral water.

"Baptism of Desire"

Is there any "substitute" for Baptism with water?

If through no fault of one's own, a person has not received Baptism, he can attain salvation through baptism of desire.

What is baptism of desire?

The unbaptized person receives baptism of desire by making an act of perfect contrition or of charity (i.e., by expressing sorrow for all serious personal sins, professing love for God above all things, and wanting to do His will in all that is necessary for salvation).

This baptism of desire is termed such because the chief effects produced are those of Baptism by water: both original and personal sin are removed, sanctifying grace is infused and one becomes a child of God and an heir to heaven. However, the sacramental seal is not imprinted, nor does this baptism establish membership in Christ's visible Church, with a right to receive other sacraments.

What is baptism of blood?

Baptism of blood is the reception of grace by an unbaptized person because he or she gives his or her life for love of Christ or a Christian virtue.

What are the requirements for baptism of blood?

For baptism of blood (martyrdom) it is necessary that the unbaptized person undergo death, or sufferings which would normally cause death. The person who inflicts the mortal action must do so because of opposition to the Catholic Church, the Faith, or one of the Christian virtues.

Does baptism of desire lessen the importance of spreading the Gospel?

No, for without religious instruction, the sacraments and the witness of Christian companions, it is very difficult to keep God's grace and grow in it. Vatican II declared: "A necessity lies upon the Church and at the same time a sacred duty to preach the Gospel.... The members of the Church are impelled to carry on such missionary activity by reason of the love with which they love God and by which they desire to share with all men the spiritual goods of both this life and the life to come" (Decree on the Mission Activity of the Church, no. 7).

The Baptismal Rite

What does the rite of Baptism include?

The baptismal ceremony is a joyous celebration— the welcoming of a new member into the family of God. Whenever possible it is held on a Sunday. The parents are present. Together with the sponsors, relatives and friends, they participate in a meaningful rite that includes one or more readings from Scripture, a prayer of the faithful, the litany of the saints and other prayers, including a renewal of the baptismal promises. The person to be baptized is anointed with the oil of catechumens, symbolizing strength for life's combat. Then, at the moment of Baptism, water is poured on the person's head while the words are said: "I baptize you in the name of the Father and of the Son and of the Holy Spirit." It is at this moment that the infant, child or adult becomes an adopted son or daughter of God.

The newly baptized is anointed with sacred chrism, to show his new relationship to Christ, Priest and King.* This anointing symbolizes the imprinting of the sacramental character, which took place a few moments earlier in the Baptism itself. He receives a white robe that represents his baptismal innocence and a burning candle, which stands for the light of faith.

Baptism is not always given by pouring (infusion). It may also be given by immersion (at least of the crown of the head).

Baptism's Far-Reaching Effects

What are the effects of Baptism?

By Baptism we are set free from original sin and made children of God (His very temples) and heirs to eternal life. We also become members of the Church, for the baptismal character makes us members of Christ's Mystical Body, which is the Church, and enables us to receive the other sacraments. (Also, adults who receive Baptism with sorrow for sin are cleansed of all personal sin.)

Is Baptism necessary for salvation?

Christ said:

"I solemnly assure you,
no one can enter into God's kingdom
without being begotten of water and Spirit" (John 3:5).

"In explicit terms Christ Himself affirmed the necessity of faith and Baptism...and thereby affirmed also the necessity of the Church, for through Baptism as through a door, men enter the Church. Whosoever,

---

*In ancient times, kings, priests and prophets were anointed— signed with oil—as an indication of their consecration. The baptized person begins to share in the royal priesthood of Christ.

therefore, knowing that the Catholic Church was made necessary by Christ, would refuse to enter it or to remain in it, could not be saved" (Constitution on the Church, no. 14).

Baptism—administered with water or received by desire or blood—is essential for salvation.

Does Baptism automatically bring us to salvation?

No (unless we die as infants), because, while all guilt of sin is removed in Baptism, we are still left with the infirmity of our fallen nature. It is up to us to pray and to make use of the graces received in Baptism in order to avoid evil and lead holy lives. Christ asks all His followers to imitate Him in unceasingly doing good to others: "Your light must shine before men so that they may see goodness in your acts and give praise to your heavenly Father" (Matthew 5:16).

But the battle which every baptized Catholic must fight against the world, the flesh and the devil is nothing compared with the eternal reward which God has promised to His faithful children.

"Eye has not seen, ear has not heard,
    nor has it so much as dawned on man
    what God has prepared for those who love him"
(1 Corinthians 2:9).

Re-Baptism?

Can a person be baptized more than once?

Because the effects of Baptism are lasting, the baptized person is a Christian forever. Baptism establishes a permanent relationship with Christ, and this relationship can never be erased. This relationship may be called the seal or character of the sacrament. It is a special quality by which Christ will know His followers and by which we share in His royal priesthood. Therefore, a Christian is baptized only once.

If a person is baptized in a non-Catholic religion, must he be baptized again in the Catholic Church to become a member?

If the original Baptism was valid, it cannot be repeated, even conditionally. Very many non-Catholic Baptisms are perfectly valid.

What is conditional Baptism?

Conditional Baptism is given when it is uncertain whether a person has been baptized or when there is a fear that the sacrament might have been administered improperly.

The Sacrament of Baptism cannot be repeated, and therefore to baptize conditionally is not allowed unless there is prudent doubt of the fact or validity of a baptism already administered.

Is "Baptism of the Holy Spirit" necessary or useful for salvation?

When a person is baptized, he is baptized in the name of the Blessed Trinity—Father, Son and Holy Spirit—according to Christ's command:

> "Full authority has been given to me
> both in heaven and on earth;
> go, therefore, and make disciples of all the
>   nations.
> Baptize them in the name
> 'of the Father,
> and of the Son,
> and of the Holy Spirit' " (Matthew 28:18-19).

Since we can be baptized only once, a separate baptism or second baptism of the Holy Spirit (apart from the reception of the Holy Spirit in a special way at Confirmation) is not a sacrament; neither is it necessary or useful for salvation.

The Baptismal Promises

What are the baptismal promises?

The baptismal promises are promises to renounce the devil and to live according to the teachings of Christ and His Church. We renew these promises at Easter. It is well also to renew them frequently throughout the year, to remind ourselves of what our Christian commitment involves.

Paul VI on the Dignity of the Baptized

"It is necessary to restore to holy Baptism, that is, to the fact of having been incorporated by means of this sacrament into the Mystical Body of Christ, which is the Church, all of its significance. It is specially important that the baptized person should have a highly conscious esteem of his elevation, or, rather, of his rebirth to the most happy reality of being an adopted son of God, to the dignity of being a brother of Christ, to the good fortune, we mean to the grace and joy of the indwelling of the Holy Spirit, to the vocation to a new life....

"To be Christians, to have received holy Baptism, must not be looked upon as something indifferent or of little importance, but it must be imprinted deeply and happily in the conscience of every baptized person. He must truly look upon it, as did the Christians of old, as an "illumination," which, by drawing down upon him the life-giving ray of divine Truth, opens heaven to him, sheds light upon earthly life and enables him to walk as a child of the light towards the vision of God, the spring of eternal happiness" *(Paths of the Church, no. 39).*

Confirmation

The Sacrament and Its Origin

What is Confirmation?

Confirmation is the sacrament of strength. Through the coming of the Holy Spirit one is given the spiritual strength to profess, live and witness to the Catholic Faith as a true apostle of Jesus Christ.

What does "confirm" mean?

To confirm means to strengthen. In Confirmation our faith is deepened and strengthened, and through this sacrament we are more perfectly bound to Christ and to His Church.

Are there Old Testament references to the Sacrament of Confirmation?

The prophets Joel, Isaiah and Ezekiel spoke of the outpouring of the Spirit upon men:

> "...I will pour out
>   my spirit upon all mankind" (Joel 3:1).

> "I will pour out water upon the thirsty ground,
>   and streams upon the dry land;
> I will pour out my spirit upon your offspring,
>   and my blessing upon your descendants"
>   (Isaiah 44:3).

> "No longer will I hide my face from them, for I have poured out my spirit upon the house of Israel, says the Lord God" (Ezekiel 39:29).

The Spirit which the prophets spoke of comes to us in a most special way in the Sacrament of Confirmation.

Are we sure that the Sacrament of Confirmation was instituted by Christ?

Yes. Although we are uncertain of the time and circumstances of the institution we know that Christ gave us this sacrament before ascending into heaven, since the Apostles administered it after Pentecost.

That Christ instituted the Sacrament of Confirmation is a dogma of faith.

Did Christ speak of this sacrament?

Jesus Christ referred many times to the gift of the Spirit:

> "I will ask the Father
> and he will give you another Paraclete—
> to be with you always..." (John 14:16).

> "...The Paraclete, the Holy Spirit
> whom the Father will send in my name,
> will instruct you in everything,
> and remind you of all that I told you"
>   (John 14:26; see also John 16:7f.; Luke 24:49; Acts 1:5).

Did Christ promise the Holy Spirit only to the Apostles?

The Apostles received the Spirit on Pentecost (cf. Acts 2:4). However, Christ also intended that *each* member of His Church be filled with the Holy Spirit.

St. Peter proclaimed this fact after his discourse on Pentecost:

> "You must reform and be baptized, each one of you, in the name of Jesus Christ, that your sins may be forgiven; then you will receive the gift of the Holy Spirit. It was to you and your children that the promise was made, and to all those still far off whom the Lord our God calls" (Acts 2:38-39).

Where in Scripture do we find proof that the Apostles administered the Sacrament of Confirmation?

We find two records of this in the Acts of the Apostles:

> "Philip went down to the town of Samaria and there proclaimed the Messiah.... When the apostles in Jerusalem heard that Samaria had accepted the word of God, they sent Peter and John to them. The two went down to these people and prayed that they might receive the Holy Spirit. It had not as yet come down upon them since they had only been baptized in the name of the Lord Jesus. The pair upon arriving imposed hands on them and they received the Holy Spirit" (Acts 8:5, 14-17).

> "They were baptized in the name of the Lord Jesus. As Paul laid his hands on them, the Holy Spirit came down on them and they began to speak in tongues and to utter prophecies" (Acts 19:5-6).

The Minister and the Recipient

Who is the minister of Confirmation?

The bishop is the ordinary minister of Confirmation. Bishops are the successors of the Apostles and leaders in the Church. In the Church's name the bishop sends confirmed Christians out on a mission—to spread the Faith by word and example. Priests may confirm in certain circumstances.

Who may receive Confirmation?

Any baptized Catholic who is not already confirmed may receive Confirmation and is obliged to do so.

In some rites, Confirmation is given immediately after Baptism. In the Latin rite, the sacrament is to be conferred at about the age of reason, unless the bishops' conference determines another age or the person is in danger of death.

(Adults who have not received Confirmation are obliged to do so.)

What is necessary to receive this sacrament worthily?

Those who have attained the use of reason must be in the state of grace, have suitable instruction* and be able to renew their baptismal promises.

Is Confirmation valid if received while not in the state of grace?

If the person being confirmed is not in the state of grace, he commits a serious sin of sacrilege. The sacrament is valid, but the person confirmed will not receive the graces of Confirmation until he regains the state of grace.

The "Sign" of Confirmation

What is the sacramental sign of Confirmation?

The anointing of the forehead with sacred chrism, done by the laying on of the hand, together with the words, "_____, be sealed with the Gift of the Holy Spirit," constitute the sign of Confirmation.

What is the significance of the anointing of the forehead in the form of a cross?

The anointing in the form of a cross signifies a spiritual seal that the Spirit bestows (the character of Confirmation), which makes the confirmed more like Christ. The confirmed now shares more fully in Christ's priesthood and in His prophetic mission; he is Christ's witness. The cross also stands for the Faith which we must profess. It is placed on the forehead because we must be *proud* to profess it openly.

What is sacred chrism?

Chrism is a mixture of olive or vegetable oil and some aromatic substance that is blessed by the bishop on Holy Thursday.

---

*The appendices of this book summarize the chief truths and duties of our Faith.

What does chrism signify?

Chrism is very symbolic because it contains a sweet scented aromatic substance whose odor quickly spreads. This stands for the way goodness and holiness "spread" and influence others. It also stands for freedom from sin. The oil itself stands for strength.

What is the meaning of the laying on of hands* that takes place a few moments before the anointing?

This gesture reminds us that the Holy Spirit is about to be conferred through the bishop (or priest) confirming. The Apostles confirmed by a laying on of hands.

The Graces of Confirmation

What are the effects of the Sacrament of Confirmation?

The main effects are an increase of the divine life of grace in those who place no obstacle, a special sacramental grace and a lasting spiritual seal or character. These effects are accompanied by growth in the infused virtues of faith, hope and charity, which enable us to believe in God, to trust His promises and to love Him and others for His sake.

The Holy Spirit also gives us a greater abundance of His seven gifts:

wisdom
understanding
right judgment (counsel)
courage (fortitude)
knowledge
reverence (piety)
wonder and awe (fear of the Lord).

---

* In this gesture the bishop (or the priest who will confirm if no bishop is present) and the concelebrating priests extend their hands over those to be confirmed.

What is the sacramental grace of Confirmation?

The sacramental grace of Confirmation is a strength or power that enables the confirmed to believe firmly and to live up to his or her Faith bravely. This grace gives the confirmed the "right" to future actual graces (light and strength from the Holy Spirit) necessary for conserving, defending and sharing the Faith.

If we are given this strength in Confirmation, why is it that we still fall into sin?

Confirmation does strengthen us, as do the other sacraments. But it must be remembered that we have free will. Therefore it is up to us to courageously choose to do good with the graces received through the sacraments.

What is the character of Confirmation?

This character is a spiritual and lasting seal that marks the Christian as a witness of Christ. Through the character a Catholic is more perfectly bound to the Church, shares more fully in Christ's priesthood and begins to share in His prophetic mission.

Is it necessary to receive the Sacrament of Confirmation?

Even though Confirmation is not absolutely necessary for salvation, to deliberately neglect receiving the sacrament could be a serious matter, since the Church obliges us to receive Confirmation and one who fails to do so deprives himself of a special sacramental grace which will enable him by word and example to continue Christ's mission on earth as a responsible member of His Mystical Body.

Preparation for Confirmation

How should one prepare to receive Confirmation?

The candidate for Confirmation should review the chief truths and duties of the Faith and try to understand and live them. He should be in the state of grace, and should resolve to live a deeply Christian life. He should pray fervently to the Holy Spirit, asking for His seven gifts and the greatest blessings possible. The Apostles in the Cenacle "devoted themselves to constant prayer" (Acts 1:14), until they had been "clothed with power from on high" (Luke 24:49).

What does the Confirmation sponsor do?

The Confirmation sponsor presents the candidate and aids him in fulfilling his baptismal promises faithfully. (It is preferred that the baptismal godparent also be the Confirmation sponsor. In any case the same conditions apply as for the baptismal sponsor.)

Confirmation and Responsibility

Why is Confirmation a sacrament of initiation?

Confirmation is a sacrament of initiation because by it the baptized Catholic becomes a "full-fledged member of the Church" and must therefore defend it and proclaim its teachings to others.

Is a person assured of salvation just because he is confirmed?

Those who are confirmed are not sure of being saved, for they are still free. The grace of God received in Confirmation or in any other sacrament does not destroy freedom. However, we are never in the right when we choose to do wrong and disobey God's commandments, for this is to abuse the gift of freedom. God made us free in order that we would choose good.

What does it mean to witness to Christ?

To witness to Christ means to live our Christian vocation to the best of our ability. This also means to love it and try to make ourselves, first of all, true followers of the Lord. We will want to share our Catholic Faith with others who may not know it, or who may have forgotten it. We do this by performing the works of mercy, by receiving Penance and the Holy Eucharist frequently, by praying for everyone, by giving good example in the practice of virtue and observance of the commandments, by openly declaring our Faith when it would be wrong to remain silent, by trying to draw others to Christ, by offering our sufferings to God, by studying the Catholic Faith more earnestly, by refusing to read anything that would endanger our faith or morals, by aiding the missions with prayer and alms, and by encouraging vocations to the priesthood and religious life.

"All sons of the Church should have a lively awareness of their responsibility to the world; they should foster in themselves a truly catholic spirit; they should spend their forces in the work of evangelization. And yet, let everyone know that his first and most important obligation for the spread of the Faith is this: to lead a profoundly Christian life" (Decree on the Mission Activity of the Church, no. 36).

What are some ways a confirmed Catholic may participate in the evangelization of the world?

Docile, tactful and enthusiastic members are urgently needed by many organizations on local, parish, diocesan, regional, national and international levels: CCD, the Legion of Mary, Catholic parent groups, secular institutes (consecrated life in the world), pro-life movements, Church-sponsored or secular groups founded to help the neglected and the elderly, to prevent discrimination, to improve the standards of local theaters...and so the list continues. Whatever we do, wherever we go, in the least significant of our actions, we who are confirmed bear within ourselves the seal of the Spirit; because of this seal, we are Christ's instruments in leavening society with Christ's message, in preparing people for the reception of grace. The far-reaching effects of our actions and words derive from the sacramental seal—which Christ, through His Holy Spirit, has bestowed on His witnesses.

> "You are the light of the world. A city set on a hill cannot be hidden. Men do not light a lamp and then put it under a bushel basket. They set it on a stand where it gives light to all in the house. In the same way, your light must shine before men so that they may see goodness in your acts and give praise to your heavenly Father" (Matthew 5:14-16).

Is it necessary for the Church to evangelize?

"...The presentation of the Gospel message is not an optional contribution for the Church. It is the duty incumbent on her by the command of the Lord Jesus, so that people can believe and be saved. This message is necessary. It is unique. It cannot be replaced. It does not permit either indifference, syncretism or accommodation. It is a question of people's salvation. It is the beauty of revelation that it represents. It brings with it a wisdom that is not of this world. It is able to stir up by itself faith—faith that rests on the power of God. It is truth. It merits having the apostle consecrate to it all his time and all his energies, and to sacrifice for it, if necessary, his own life" (Paul VI, On Evangelization in the Modern World, no. 5).

"All Christians, wherever they live, are bound to show forth, by the example of their lives and by the witness of the word, that new man put on at Baptism and the power of the Holy Spirit by which they have been strengthened at Confirmation. Thus other men, observing their good works, can glorify the Father (cf. Matthew 5:16) and can perceive more fully the real meaning of human life and the universal bond of the community of mankind" (Decree on the Mission Activity of the Church, no. 11).

Paul VI on Confirmation

"On the day of the feast of Pentecost, the Holy Spirit came down in an extraordinary way on the Apostles as they were gathered together with Mary the Mother of Jesus and the group of disciples. They were so 'filled with' the Holy Spirit (Acts 2:4) that by divine inspiration they began to proclaim 'the mighty works of God.' Peter regarded the Spirit who had thus come down upon the Apostles as the gift of the messianic age (cf. Acts 2:17-18). Those who believed the Apostles' preaching were then baptized and they too received 'the gift of the Holy Spirit' (Acts 2:38). From that time on the Apostles, in fulfillment of Christ's wish, imparted the gift of the Spirit to the newly baptized by the laying on of hands to complete the grace of Baptism. Hence it is that the Letter to the Hebrews lists among the first elements of Christian instruction the teaching about baptisms and the laying on of hands (Hebrews 6:2). This laying on of hands is rightly recognized by Catholic tradition as the beginning of the Sacrament of Confirmation, which in a certain way perpetuates the grace of Pentecost in the Church.

"This makes clear the specific importance of Confirmation for sacramental initiation by which the faithful 'as members of the living Christ are incorporated into Him and made like Him through Baptism and through Confirmation and the Eucharist.' In Baptism, the newly baptized receive forgiveness of sins, adoption as sons of God, and the character of Christ, by which they are made members of the Church and for the first time become sharers in the priesthood of their Savior (cf. 1 Peter 2:5, 9). Through the Sacrament of Confirmation, those who have been born anew in Baptism receive the inexpressible Gift, the Holy Spirit Himself, by which 'they are endowed... with special strength.' Moreover, having received the character of this sacrament, they are 'bound more intimately to the Church' and 'they are more strictly obliged to spread and defend the Faith both by word and by deed as true witnesses of Christ.' Finally, Confirmation is so closely linked with the Holy Eucharist that the faithful, after being signed by holy Baptism and Confirmation, are incorporated fully into the Body of Christ by participation in the Eucharist" (Paul VI, Apostolic Constitution on the Sacrament of Confirmation).

Holy Eucharist

The Sacrament and Its Origin

What is the Holy Eucharist?

The Holy Eucharist is both a sacrifice, pertaining to the essence of the Mass, and a sacrament in which our Lord Jesus Christ, body, blood, soul and divinity, is received by the faithful under the appearances of bread and wine.

The Holy Eucharist is the heart of Catholic life and worship, because the Son of God is truly present in the Blessed Sacrament for us to adore, offer and receive.

Because of all these realities, the Eucharist has been described as a "sacrifice-sacrament, a communion-sacrament, and a presence-sacrament."[*]

Why did Jesus Christ institute the Sacrament of the Holy Eucharist?

Out of love, Jesus Christ instituted the Holy Eucharist in order to renew His sacrifice and thus apply the fruits of His redemption to all, throughout the centuries. He also instituted the Eucharist to strengthen us and remain with us always. After His resurrection, Jesus was to return to His Father. But His infinite love and power created a means—the Holy Eucharist—by which He could still remain on earth, not in one place but in every church, to be the intimate friend and companion of His people.

---

[*]John Paul II, *Redeemer of Man*, no. 20.

When did Jesus institute the Holy Eucharist?

Jesus Christ instituted the Holy Eucharist at the Last Supper, the night before He died. Jesus took bread, blessed and broke it, and gave it to His disciples, saying, "Take this and eat it, this is my body." Then He took a cup of wine, blessed it and gave it to them, saying, "All of you must drink from it, for this is my blood..." (Matthew 26:26-28). He commissioned His Apostles, "Do this as a remembrance of me" (Luke 22:19), thereby giving them and their successors the power to change bread and wine into His Body and Blood.

Christ's Real Presence

Can we be sure that Jesus meant His words, "This is my body; this is my blood," to be taken literally?

Yes, we can.

First, let us consider what the Church teaches about these words. She professes and proclaims that Jesus Christ—true God and true Man—is really present in the Holy Eucharist. And the Church has taught this down through the centuries. Because Jesus promised that His presence (cf. Matthew 28:20) and the guidance of the Holy Spirit (cf. John 14:16-17, 26) would be with the Church until the end of time, we can be sure that the Church's teaching on the Eucharist is *true*. God will not let His Church teach error.

Let us also turn to the Scriptures. Some scholars consider Jesus' discourse on the bread of life (John 6:26-58) as a New Testament counterpart of various Old Testament passages on the banquet prepared by divine wisdom for her disciples. But a distinction has to be made, a distinction which the Fathers of the Church were quick to point out. In verse 51, a new phrase appears in the discourse: "the bread I will give."

At that time the word "give" was used to indicate sacrifice, as in St. Paul's exclamation, "The Son of God... loved me and gave himself for me" (Galatians 2:20). From that point on, Jesus speaks of giving His *flesh* to *eat* and His *blood* to *drink*. Gone now is any resemblance to the banquet set forth by wisdom. Jesus uses terms that grate harshly on the ears of His Hebrew followers (who were forbidden to drink blood and who certainly shrank from the thought of eating human flesh). Many of them turn away, leaving only the Twelve to profess through Peter: "You have the words of eternal life" (John 6:68).

Jesus' words cannot be interpreted as *metaphors,* for He says, "real food" and "real drink" (John 6:55). Moreover, the only contemporary metaphorical use of the terms "eat someone's flesh; drink someone's blood" expressed calumniation and persecution. We cannot imagine Jesus denying eternal life to all who would not persecute Him! (cf. John 6:53)

We must also note that Jesus did not correct His listeners' interpretation, even though He lost a large number of followers by not doing so. He did not call them back and say that they had misunderstood Him; He only asked, "Does it shake your faith?" (John 6:61)

Yes, the Real Presence of Jesus Christ in the Holy Eucharist must be understood literally.

How is Jesus able to change bread and wine into His Body and Blood?

Jesus is able to change bread and wine into His Body and Blood by His almighty power. Jesus is God: He can do anything that He chooses to do. On earth He worked many miracles by His divine power. If God could create the entire universe out of nothing by a simple act of His will, can we doubt that He can also change bread and wine into His own Body and Blood?

What is transubstantiation?

Transubstantiation is the changing of the entire substance of the bread and wine into Christ's Body and Blood. This takes place at Mass at the words of consecration, when the priest says, "This is my body.... This is the cup of my blood."

The "Sign" of the Eucharist

What is the "sign" of the Eucharist?

The "sign" of the Eucharist consists of the appearances of bread and wine, together with the "words of institution"—that is, the words of Jesus that are repeated at the consecration of every Mass. After the priest says the words, our Savior becomes present. The substance of bread and wine are no longer there; only their appearances remain.

Does Christ truly become present no matter what kind of bread and wine are prepared for the Mass?

No. Therefore, the Church's specifications must be followed. The bread is to be made only from wheat flour and water; the wine is to be grape wine. In the Latin rite, further, the bread is to be unleavened, but this last is for lawfulness, not for validity.

The Names of This Sacrament

Why is this sacrament called the Eucharist?

This sacrament is called the Eucharist, that is, "thanksgiving," because of the thanks Jesus offered to the Father at the Last Supper before He consecrated the bread and wine. St. Paul recalls the moment for us: "I received from the Lord what I handed on to you, namely, that the Lord Jesus on the night in which he was betrayed took bread, and after he had given thanks, broke it and said, 'This is my body, which is for you. Do this in remembrance of me.' In the same way, after the supper, he took the cup, saying, 'This cup is the new covenant in my blood. Do this, whenever you drink it, in remembrance of me.' Every time, then, you eat this bread and drink this cup, you proclaim the death of the Lord until he comes!" (1 Corinthians 11:23-26)

The Mass is also the highest means by which we can carry out our duty of giving thanks to God.

By what other names is the Holy Eucharist known?

The Holy Eucharist is called the Blessed Sacrament because It is the center and summit of all the sacraments; in It, Christ Himself is present, whole and entire, God and Man. When received by the faithful, the Eucharist is called Holy Communion. It is called Holy Viaticum when It is received by those who are dangerously ill or near death.

The Eucharistic Celebration

What is the Mass?

The Mass or Eucharistic Celebration is the renewal of the sacrifice of the cross. In the Mass Christ offers Himself to the Father under the appearances of bread and wine. It is a sacred banquet in which the People of God receive Jesus, the Bread of Life. The Mass is also a memorial of Jesus' death, resurrection and ascension.

What is meant by "sacrifice"?

Sacrifice is the offering of a victim or gift by a priest to God alone and is accomplished by the destruction of the offering in some way.

What is the purpose of sacrifice?

Sacrifice is a way of adoring God—of acknowledging His supreme dominion over the universe and our complete dependence on Him and submission to the divine will. Through sacrifice we also seek to make reparation to God for our offenses, to show our gratitude for His great goodness and to ask Him for favors.

Is sacrifice something foreign to the nature of man?

No. From the beginning of human history men have offered sacrifices to God. The destruction of the material object is a symbol of the interior offering of oneself.

Can anyone offer sacrifice?

Personal sacrifice of our own will and desires, of our time, of other things that mean much to us can and should be offered to God by everyone—all year round and especially during the penitential season of Lent. But solemn religious sacrifices are offered only by priests. The Mass, the sacrifice par excellence, can be offered only by a validly ordained priest, through whom Christ acts.

Why was Jesus' sacrifice on the cross the most perfect of all sacrifices?

The perfection of Jesus' sacrifice stems from His identity as God-Man. Sin is an infinite offense to God, because of His infinite dignity. According to strict justice, only a divine Person who had assumed a human nature could atone for such an offense by performing some act of reparation. Jesus, however, did not choose a small act of reparation, but rather allowed Himself to suffer excruciating psychic and physical pain in order to show us God's love for man and His hatred for sin.

This total sacrifice of God's beloved Son could not be other than perfect.

Is the Mass the same sacrifice as that of the cross?

Yes. The sacrifice of the Mass, carried out in obedience to Jesus' words: "Do this in memory of me," is actually the renewal of the sacrifice of Calvary. Christ is the principal priest in the Mass and He is also the

Victim. Although He does not suffer again, because the Eucharist is the risen Christ and His body is no longer subject to suffering, He *offers* Himself again to the Father with the same spirit of total self-giving that was His at the Last Supper and on Calvary. The essence of sacrifice is in the offering; thus, the Mass is the same sacrifice as that of the cross.

How can we see that the Mass is a sacrifice?

The Mass is offered on an altar, as sacrifices have been down through man's history. Many words and phrases used in the Eucharistic prayer indicate the sacrificial nature of the Mass. And the separate consecrations show us the sacrifice sacramentally, that is, through signs: the appearances of bread are a sign of Christ's Body and the appearances of wine are a sign of His Blood. They are separated mystically in the Mass as they were separated really on the cross.

For what purposes is the Mass offered?

The Mass is offered to adore God as our Creator, to thank Him for His goodness, to ask His blessings for ourselves and all mankind (living and deceased) and to satisfy His justice, which has been offended because of our sins and the sins of others. At Mass, the fruits of Christ's sacrifice are applied to us and those for whom we pray.

The Mass accomplishes all this far better than any other prayer or sacrifice could because it is the offering of Christ Himself. It is the only worthy sacrifice we can offer to God.

Our Participation in the Mass

Why should we participate in the Mass?

As God's creatures, we owe Him our worship, our adoration. The Mass is the most perfect act of worship we can offer to God, because in it we offer Him His own beloved Son. And Jesus, in our name, offers His Father adoration, praise and thanksgiving, as well as reparation for our sins.

How should we participate in the Mass?

We should participate in the Mass with careful attention and devotion, with as clear an understanding as possible of what is taking place, uniting ourselves with Christ as He offers Himself and ourselves to the heavenly Father.

In the words of Vatican II:

"The Church...earnestly desires that Christ's faithful, when present at this mystery of faith, should not be there as strangers or silent spectators; on the contrary, through a good understanding of the rites and prayers they should take part in the sacred action conscious of what they are doing, with devotion and full collaboration. They should be instructed by God's Word and be nourished at the table of the Lord's Body; they should give thanks to God; by offering the Immaculate Victim, not only through the hands of the priest, but also with him, they should learn also to offer themselves; through Christ the Mediator, they should be drawn day by day into ever more perfect union with God and with each other, so that finally God may be all in all...." (Constitution on the Sacred Liturgy, no. 48).

It should be noted, however, that it is not lawful for deacons and lay persons to say prayers—particularly the Eucharistic prayer—or perform actions proper to the celebrating priest.

"To promote active participation, the people should be encouraged to take part by means of acclamations, responses, psalmody, antiphons, and songs, as well as by actions, gestures, and bodily attitudes.

And at the proper times all should observe a reverent silence" (Constitution on the Sacred Liturgy, no. 30).

Are Catholics obliged to go to Mass?

Yes. Catholics are obliged to go to Mass on all Sundays and holy days of obligation (or the evenings preceding these days when permitted).

Do we really need to participate in the Mass from beginning to end?

Yes we do, especially on Sundays and holy days of obligation. Moreover, as we have seen, this is not to be merely a physical presence at the Mass, but an active participation of body and soul.

Have the liturgical changes affected the essential reality of the Mass in any way?

The liturgical changes which Vatican II called for, and which were completed a few years after the Council, neither destroy nor diminish the sacrifice of the Mass. Rather, when the Church's norms regarding them are followed, these changes strengthen our faith and devotion by increasing our active participation in the Mass.

The use of the local language is one of the changes that fosters participation. (However, the Latin Mass is not "out of date," provided that the Mass is said in accord with the new liturgical books.)

Actually, many of the recent "changes" were not innovations. Rather, they brought back ancient liturgical texts used by the early Christians.

The Eucharistic Lord is equally present for us as He was for our forbears. We have but to believe and to trust in the guidance of holy Mother Church, advancing not ahead of her, nor behind her, but always *with* her. Christ promised to be with the Church until the end of time, and it is impossible that Christ would allow the Church to be misled in this, the central mystery of our Faith.

The Benefits of the Mass

Does the holiness of the priest have any effect on the fruitfulness of the sacrifice of the Mass?

No, for Christ is the principal Priest and the Victim; the priest is only Christ's minister—His instrument. As long as the priest intends to consecrate the bread and wine and says the words of institution as the Church prescribes, the Mass is valid and the faithful will be able to draw fruit from it according to their dispositions. As St. John Chrysostom once wrote: "This sacrifice, no matter who offers it, be it Peter or Paul, is always the same as that which Christ gave His disciples and which priests now offer: the offering of today is in no way inferior to that which Christ offered, because it is not men who sanctify the offering of today; it is the same Christ who sanctified His own. For just as the words which God spoke are the very same as those which the priest now speaks, so too, the oblation is the very same."

What are the principal benefits of participation in the Mass?

By participation in the Mass, and especially through the reception of Holy Communion, we profit through the abundance of graces made available in every Mass: that is, an increase of sanctifying grace, of supernatural faith, hope and charity, and of the gifts and fruits of the Holy Spirit. We also obtain, if necessary, the grace to repent of mortal sin and the forgiveness of venial sins for which we are sorry, together with the remission of temporal punishment.

Should a person go to Mass even if he doesn't seem to "get anything out of it"?

The Mass has an intrinsic value, by which the fruits of the redemption are applied to our souls whether we feel anything or not. We can ask for these gifts and graces and actually receive them without feeling any sensible consolation at all. But, more important, participation in the Mass is our duty. God has given us everything; we owe Him praise, thanksgiving and reparation. And, as limited creatures, we need to ask His help, so that we may serve Him well.

Is it hypocritical to go to Mass if one is not holy and good?

No one is holy or worthy enough to receive Christ. God alone is worthy. But that is precisely why God sent His Son to atone for our sins and give us life. Jesus told us, "I have come to call, not the self-righteous, but sinners" (Matthew 9:13). We are all sinners, and therefore we all need the graces of the Mass.

Is it not just as beneficial to pray at home, since God is everywhere?

It is true that God is everywhere. Yet it is God Himself who has given us the commandment: Remember to keep holy the Lord's day. And from the first generation of Christianity, the Church has gathered for weekly worship on the day dedicated to the Lord. Moreover, as we have seen, benefits come from the Mass in great abundance because in the Mass Christ Himself prays for us.

Catholics should not cut themselves off from the Eucharistic Celebration. Even persons who cannot receive the sacraments (for example, because of divorce with remarriage) should take part in the Mass to ask God's mercy and help.

Communion and Our Responsibilities

Why do we call the reception of Jesus in the Eucharist "Holy Communion"?

Communion means "union with" or "sharing together." When we receive the Eucharist, we are united with Jesus and we participate more fully in His life of grace:

"I am the vine, you are the branches.
He who lives in me and I in him,
will produce abundantly..." (John 15:5).

At what age should children receive First Communion?

Children should receive First Communion when they have reached the age of reason. They are to be correctly prepared beforehand, and their First Communion is to be preceded by sacramental confession.

Are all Catholics obliged to receive Holy Communion?

All Catholics, from the time of First Communion on, are obliged to receive Holy Communion at least once a year. This precept must be fulfilled during the Easter time, unless it is fulfilled for a just reason at some other time during the year.

Also, any Catholic in danger of death from any cause is to receive the comfort and strength of Holy Communion as Viaticum. (Viaticum should be received even if one has gone to Communion on the same day.)

Is it necessary to receive the Sacrament of Reconciliation before every reception of Communion?

No, provided that no mortal sin has been committed since one's last confession. Anyone who knowingly and willingly receives Holy Communion in the state of mortal sin commits the grave sin of sacrilege.

The Church encourages frequent use of the Sacrament of Penance, but she does not require it before each Communion. We do not receive the Eucharist because we *are* good, but because we want to *become* good.

How long must one fast before receiving Holy Communion?

The Church requires a fast of one hour from all solid foods and liquids, both alcoholic and non-alcoholic (with the exception of water, which can be taken at any time, and medicine).

Are there any exceptions to the Eucharistic fast?

The sick and aged, even though not confined to a bed or a home, need not fast. The same holds for persons caring for them.

How should we prepare to receive the Body and Blood of Christ?

It is good to approach the Eucharist with sorrow for our sins and sentiments of faith, hope and love. For example:

"Jesus, my Savior, I am sorry for having offended You."

"Jesus, eternal Truth, I believe that You are really present in the sacred Host. Increase my faith!"

"Jesus, sole Way of salvation, though I am so unworthy to receive You, I trust in Your infinite mercy. Just say the word, and I will be healed."

"Jesus, Life of the world, nourish me by making Yourself my food, so that I may have the strength to serve You well."

Should we make a sign of reverence before receiving the Holy Eucharist?

Someone who receives Communion kneeling is already manifesting reverence. Those who receive standing are encouraged to make some sign of reverence—for example, a bow of the head before stepping forward to receive.

Reverence also extends to the *manner of receiving.* If one receives on the tongue, the tongue should be well extended; if in the hand, the hands should be held close to the ciborium and properly cupped. Taking the proper positions prevents such accidents as the dropping of the Host on the floor. (One who receives in the hand should step aside and consume the Host at once.)

Also, when receiving Communion in the hand, we should heed the words of St. Cyril of Jerusalem: "Consume It, making sure that not a particle is wasted.... Tell me, if you were given some gold dust, would you not hold it very carefully for fear of letting any of it fall and losing it? How much more careful, then, you should be not to let fall even a crumb of Something more precious than gold or jewels!"

May one of the faithful take the Host from the ciborium or pick up the chalice himself?

Neither of these practices is permitted to those who are not ministers of the Eucharist. Neither, therefore, may the faithful pass the ciborium or the chalice to one another.

Why do we say "Amen" just before receiving the Eucharist?

"Amen" in this context means: "So it is." In other words: "Yes, I *know* that this is the Body of Christ." Our "Amen" is an act of faith in the Real Presence of the God-Man in the Eucharist.

What Communion Does for Us

What are the effects of Holy Communion?

Holy Communion:

—draws us closer to God and His people;

—makes us grow in sanctifying grace;

—guards us against falling into mortal sin;

—obtains forgiveness of the venial sins for which we are sorry;

—remits the temporal punishment due to venial sin;

—enables us more easily to practice good works.

How does Communion unite us with Christ?

Holy Communion unites us with Christ in a special bond of love. It is a total union of our mind, will, heart and body with the mind, will, heart and body of Christ. Although the physical union lasts only a few minutes, the resulting spiritual union is to continue throughout our lives.

How does this sacrament unite us with one another?

We are united with one another through our sacramental union with Christ. Vatican II explains: "By reason of the offering and through Holy Communion, all take part in the liturgical service.... Strengthened in Holy Communion by the Body of Christ, they then manifest in a concrete way that unity of the People of God which is suitably signified and wondrously brought about by this most august sacrament" (Constitution on the Sacred Liturgy, no. 11).

What are some other effects of Holy Communion?

The Eucharist is food for God's people on pilgrimage to eternity. What the angel said to Elijah, we can apply to the frequent reception of Communion: "Get up and eat, else the journey will be too long for you" (1 Kings 19:7). The Eucharist is the nourishment not only of individual souls but also of the entire Christian community. It is both a sign and the source of love that unites and sustains the Mystical Body.

The Eucharist is a remedy for our weaknesses, and healing for our spiritual miseries. By It we are forgiven the venial sins for which we are sorry, and we are strengthened in our combat against evil. Faith, hope and love take stronger root within us, and we are able to understand, love and live our Faith better.

The Eucharist is also a pledge of future glory—our eternal union with Christ in the happiness of heaven— a glory of the body as well as of the soul:

"He who feeds on my flesh
and drinks my blood
has life eternal,
and I will raise him up on the last day" (John 6:54).

Is Holy Communion necessary for salvation?

Jesus said:

"Let me solemnly assure you,
if you do not eat the flesh of the Son of Man
and drink his blood,
you have no life in you" (John 6:53).

Therefore, in concern for our salvation, the Church has commanded that we receive Holy Communion at least once a year. But she earnestly recommends that we receive Holy Communion very often, even daily, if possible. (Indeed, we may receive at every Mass in which we participate.) Just as we need to nourish ourselves with material food each day in order to stay alive, so, too, we need Christ in the Eucharist —the spiritual food of our souls—if we wish to grow in His grace and live up to the demands of our Faith in a secular world.

What are the advantages of frequent Communion?

Frequent Communion increases union with Christ, nourishes the spiritual life more abundantly, strengthens the soul in virtue and gives the communicant a stronger pledge of eternal happiness.

Questions Frequently Asked

What is the purpose of Communion under both kinds?

Communion under both kinds, or species, helps us to recall Christ's sacrifice, in which His Body and Blood were physically separated on the cross. However, although we think of the appearances of bread as indicating only Christ's Body and the appearances of wine as indicating only Christ's Blood, in reality the whole Christ, risen and glorious, never to die again, is present in each consecrated host and in each portion of consecrated wine. Therefore, we can obtain all the grace of the sacrament by receiving the consecrated host alone. However, as the new Roman Missal points out: "The sign of communion is more complete when given under both kinds, since in that form, the sign of the Eucharistic meal appears more clearly."

Who may administer Communion?

Communion is normally administered by a bishop, priest or deacon, but It may also be administered by an authorized lay minister under certain conditions.

It is necessary that such a person, usually chosen by the bishop, be properly instructed and distinguish himself by Christian life, faith and morals. He is to strive to be worthy of such a great office, cultivating devotion to the Holy Eucharist and showing himself as an example to the other faithful in reverence for the Blessed Sacrament.

May the Holy Eucharist be kept on one's person or carried on a journey?

The Holy Eucharist may not be kept on one's person or carried on a journey unless there is an urgent pastoral need and the precepts of the diocesan bishop are observed.

How long does the Real Presence of Christ in the Holy Eucharist last?

The Real Presence lasts as long as the appearances of bread and wine remain. Because the appearances of wine will not remain long, the consecrated wine is to be completely consumed at each Mass. The appearances of bread remain longer, and therefore consecrated hosts are reserved in the tabernacle after Mass for Viaticum, the adoration of the faithful and for the Communion of the sick. The concept that Christ's presence leaves the consecrated hosts after Holy Communion is not a Catholic one.

Gratitude for the Eucharist

Does the Church encourage Eucharistic devotions?

The Church does encourage Eucharistic devotions, for the Eucharist is Jesus Christ Himself, human and divine, deserving of our adoration. Pope John Paul II tells us that our adoration must express itself in personal prayer before the Blessed Sacrament, Holy Hours and longer periods of exposition, Eucharistic benediction, Eucharistic processions, Eucharistic congresses, and the Corpus Christi observance. The Church also reminds us that whenever we pass before a tabernacle in which the Blessed Sacrament is reserved we should genuflect as a sign of reverence in a manner that is neither hurried nor careless.

How can we thank our Lord for the Sacrament of the Holy Eucharist?

We can thank our Lord for His presence in the Holy Eucharist by attending Mass frequently (at least once a week, and more often if possible), by receiving Holy Communion devoutly and frequently, by paying visits to our Lord in the Blessed Sacrament, and by participating in the various Eucharistic devotions held in our parishes.

The Holy Eucharist is the sign of God's infinite, abiding love for man. It is His most powerful means of pouring grace into the human soul. How we should thank God every day for instituting this Blessed Sacrament, and for our Catholic religion—by which we have received the faith to believe in the Real Presence!

John Paul II on Eucharistic Worship

"This worship is directed towards God the Father through Jesus Christ in the Holy Spirit. In the first place towards the Father, who, as St. John's Gospel says, 'loved the world so much that he gave his only Son, so that everyone who believes in him may not be lost but may have eternal life.'

"It is also directed, in the Holy Spirit, to the incarnate Son, in the economy of salvation, especially at that moment of supreme dedication and total abandonment of Himself to which the words uttered in the Upper Room refer: 'This is my body given up for you.... This is the cup of my blood shed for you....' The liturgical acclamation: 'We proclaim your death, Lord Jesus' takes us back precisely to that moment; and with the proclamation of His resurrection we embrace in the same act of veneration Christ risen and glorified 'at the right hand of the Father,' as also the expectation of His 'coming in glory.' *Yet it is the voluntary emptying of Himself, accepted by the Father and glorified with the resurrection,* which, sacramentally celebrated together with the resurrection, brings us to adore the Redeemer who 'became obedient unto death, even death on a cross.'

"And this adoration of ours contains yet another special characteristic. It is compenetrated by the greatness of that human death, in which the world, that is to say each one of us, has been loved 'to the end.' Thus it is also a response that tries to repay that love immolated even to the death on the cross: it is our 'Eucharist,' that is to say our giving Him thanks, our praise of Him for having redeemed us by His death and made us sharers in immortal life through His resurrection.

"This worship, given therefore to the Trinity of the Father and of the Son and of the Holy Spirit, above all accompanies and permeates the celebration of the Eucharistic Liturgy. But it must fill our churches also outside the timetable of Masses. Indeed, since the Eucharistic Mystery was instituted out of love, and makes Christ sacramentally present, It is worthy of thanksgiving and worship. And this worship must be prominent in all our encounters with the Blessed Sacrament, both when we visit our churches and when the sacred species are taken to the sick and administered to them.

"Adoration of Christ in this sacrament of love must also find expression *in various forms of Eucharistic devotion:* personal prayer before the Blessed Sacrament, Hours of Adoration, periods of exposition—short, prolonged and annual (Forty Hours)—Eucharistic benediction, Eucharistic processions, Eucharistic congresses. A particular mention should be made at this point of the Solemnity of the Body and Blood of Christ as an act of public worship rendered to Christ present in the Eucharist, a feast instituted by my Predecessor Urban IV in memory of the institution of this great Mystery. All this therefore corresponds to the general principles and particular norms already long in existence but newly formulated during or after the Second Vatican Council.

"The encouragement and the deepening of Eucharistic worship are *proofs of that authentic renewal* which the Council set for itself as an aim and of which they are *the central point.* And this...deserves separate reflection. The Church and the world have a great need of Eucharistic worship. Jesus waits for us in this sacrament of love. Let us be generous with our time in going to meet Him in adoration and in contemplation full of faith and ready to make reparation for the great faults and crimes of the world. May our adoration never cease" (On the Mystery and Worship of the Eucharist, no. 3).

Penance or Reconciliation

The Sacrament and Its Origin

What is Penance?

Penance is the Sacrament of Reconciliation—of God's loving forgiveness—by which we are set free from the sins committed after Baptism, free from the eternal punishment and from at least some of the temporal punishment due to sin. This sacrament helps us to grow in God's grace and strengthens us to avoid sin and lead holier lives. It also reconciles the sinner with the Church which has been wounded by his sins.

How do we know that God is willing to forgive sins?

We know that God is willing to forgive sins because in the Gospel Jesus has told us many times and in many ways that God is willing to forgive our sins. For example, He said: "The Son of Man has come to search out and save what was lost" (Luke 19:10). The Gospel of St. Luke, especially chapter 15, should be read in this light.

How do we know that Jesus forgives our sins in the Sacrament of Reconciliation?

We know this because Jesus has promised that if we are sincerely sorry for our sins, confess them to a priest, and receive absolution, we are really forgiven by God.

On Easter Sunday Jesus appeared to His Apostles and said:

"Receive the Holy Spirit.
If you forgive men's sins,
they are forgiven them;
if you hold them bound,
they are held bound" (John 20:22-23).

Questions Frequently Asked

Why is reconciliation with the Church important?

Paul VI explained this point very clearly: "Just as every personal fault of ours is reflected in our essential and vital relationship with God, so is it reflected in our relationship with the community, which is also similarly vital and connects us with the Mystical Body of Christ—the holy, living Church—of which we are all members."

Who is the minister of the Sacrament of Reconciliation?

Only a priest (not a deacon or layperson) may administer the Sacrament of Penance.

May a priest hear confessions outside his diocese?

A priest who has received from his bishop the faculty to hear confessions, may do so anywhere. Even a priest who lacks the faculty may absolve a person who is in danger of death.

Would it not be just as well to confess sins directly to God, and gain forgiveness directly?

It is admittedly much easier to do so, but certainly it is far better to abide by the method established by God Himself. Christ gave the Apostles, and through them His priests, the power to forgive sins or not. This indicates that the priest must make a judgment and therefore must know what the sins are.

The Sacrament of Reconciliation was not instituted by the Church but is of divine origin. It would be contradictory on our part to present ourselves to God to express our contrition for transgressing His law at the same time that we ignore His will by deviating from the rules He has laid down for obtaining the forgiveness of our sins.

The Fathers of the Church and other early writers stressed the necessity of confessing our sins to a priest: "The layman who falls into sin cannot by himself wash away his faults...he needs a priest" (Origen). "Sins are forgiven through the Holy Spirit certainly, but men lend Him their ministry.... They forgive sins not in their own name but in the name of the Father, the Son, and the Holy Spirit" (St. Ambrose).

Although it is possible to regain sanctifying grace by perfect contrition (sorrow because one has offended God, who is all good and deserves all our love), we can never really be sure that our contrition *is* perfect. On the other hand, we are assured that in a properly-made confession, our sins are forgiven. Moreover, any act of perfect contrition implies at least the intention to confess one's serious sins in one's next confession.

A person who has reached the age of reason is obliged to confess his serious sins at least once a year.

Should we ever be so embarrassed that we do not go to confession?

No. We must remember that the priest is Christ's representative and that he is bound by the seal of confession never to reveal anything told to him in the confessional. Nor need we fear that we will shock him by anything we may say. Also, we are free to confess to any authorized priest.

Can every sin be forgiven?

Yes, the Church's power to forgive sins includes all sins.

Does the priest ever refuse absolution?

The priest can refuse absolution to the penitent if the person is not really sorry for his serious sins or has no intention of correcting himself. Unless there is true sorrow, there is no forgiveness.

The "Sign" of Penance

What makes up the sign of Penance?

The sign of Penance is made up of three "acts of the penitent," plus the absolution given by the priest.

The penitent's three acts are: *contrition* (sorrow), *confession* and *satisfaction* (making up for the harm done when necessary and doing or saying the penance given by the priest, plus, if we wish, other penances of our own choosing).

How is the Sacrament of Reconciliation received?

The Sacrament of Reconciliation is received when we go to confession with sorrow for sin, accept the penance that the priest gives, and receive the priest's absolution, given in the name of the Blessed Trinity.

What does "absolution" mean?

Absolution means "releasing." When the priest absolves us, we are released from our sins—set free from them.

What is required in order to receive the Sacrament of Reconciliation well?

To receive the Sacrament of Reconciliation well we must:

—examine our conscience (check on our thoughts, words, actions, desires and omissions);

—have sorrow;

—be determined not to sin again;

—tell our sins in confession;

—do or say our penance.

What is a penance?

A penance is something done or accepted to make up for sin. The Bible says:

"Return to me with your whole heart,
with fasting, and weeping, and mourning" (Joel 2:12).

What Reconciliation Does for Us

What are the effects of this sacrament?

When we receive this sacrament worthily:

—our sins are forgiven;

—we are reconciled with the Church;

—our soul is restored to the state of grace (if we had committed mortal sin), or we grow in sanctifying grace (if we had committed only venial sins);

—we are set free from all the eternal punishment and at least some of the temporal punishment due to our sins;

—we receive the sacramental grace of Penance, which strengthens us to avoid sin and lead better lives in the future.

What are the rights and privileges of one who has received the Sacrament of Reconciliation?

The rights and privileges of one who has received the Sacrament of Reconciliation consist in this: a person who was in mortal sin may now receive the Eucharist and other sacraments. He has been reconciled with God and the Church, and thus is reinstated in His grace which brings one to heaven.

What are the duties of one who has received the Sacrament of Reconciliation?

One who has received the Sacrament of Reconciliation must say or do the penance given by the priest, avoid everything that would lead to sin, and make up as much as possible and necessary for the harm done.

The Examination of Conscience

What is conscience?

Conscience is a practical judgment (decision) that something is right or wrong because of the law and will of God.

What is necessary to have a correct conscience?

To have a correct conscience one first needs to know God's law (the natural law for all men, written down in the ten commandments and made more perfect by Jesus), the laws of the Church and also his particular duties as a Catholic. Then one's conscience will really express what is right or wrong in a particular situation.

How does one examine his conscience?

In an examination of conscience one recalls what wrong he has done in thoughts, words and actions as well as the duties accomplished poorly or not carried out at all. As a help, the ten commandments can be recalled one by one, as well as the special duties of Catholics and one's own particular duties.*

Mortal Sin

What is mortal sin?

Mortal sin is the greatest evil that can be imagined. Mortal sin drives God's life out of a soul, gravely offends Him, keeps one out of heaven and condemns him forever to hell, if he dies impenitent.

---

* Some helpful questions will be found in the appendix of this book.

When is a sin mortal?

There are three factors that make a sin mortal:

1) The thought, desire, word, action or omission must be seriously wrong or considered seriously wrong.

2) The person must know (or think) that it is seriously wrong.

3) The person must freely consent to it.

What is the false theory called "situation ethics"?

Situation ethics teaches that there is no fixed moral code given to human beings by the Creator. It holds that individuals must make moral choices (choices about right and wrong) according to a particular situation—that is, what is right or best in this moment *for me*. This false theory permits gravely sinful actions, and leads people who follow it down the road to despair because the human mind cannot long be pressured into calling gravely sinful matters "slight."

Is there a distinction between "grave sins" and "mortal sins," so that even though a person might commit occasional grave sins there would be no mortal guilt?

There is no such distinction. Every individual *grave* sin is *mortal*—that is, it drives God's grace out of the soul. The school of thought which teaches that if one has made a "fundamental option" (a basic choice) for God, only a series of "grave" sins can change that option and result in a state of "mortal" sin, is not in accord with Church teaching.

Are there any requirements for confessing mortal sins?

A person should say what kind of sins they were and—as far as possible—tell how many times these sins were committed, as well as any circumstances that might alter their nature. If he confesses all the mortal sins he remembers, everything will be forgiven. On the other hand, to deliberately conceal a mortal sin in confession is to commit another mortal sin, and none of the other sins are forgiven.

Can a person in mortal sin receive Communion if he makes an act of perfect contrition?

No, except in some rather rare cases.

Venial Sin

What is venial sin?

A sin is venial when one of the conditions for a mortal sin is missing. For example, the thought, desire, word, action or omission is wrong but not seriously so, or it is seriously wrong but a person does not clearly see this or does not fully consent to it.

Should we avoid venial sins?

We should avoid venial sins because even though they do not destroy the life of grace, they are an offense to God, and they weaken our friendship with Him. They also dispose us to mortal sin and merit for us some temporal punishment either in this life or in the next.

Sins of Omission

Does someone who thinks that he has not hurt anyone have any obligation regarding Penance?

Besides our negative duty of avoiding all sins against the commandments of God and the regulations of the Church, we have a moral obligation to build up the Christian community with works of a positive nature, such as: charitable deeds, the giving of good example, and the diligent fulfillment of all the duties of our state in life.

There are, then, sins of omission—meaning the failure to do what one should have done. Such sins are mortal or venial depending upon the nature of what we have failed to do.

Frequent Confession

How often should a Catholic receive the Sacrament of Reconciliation?

For motives of spiritual growth, of eliminating habits of sin and of working for perfection, a fervent Catholic may approach the Sacrament of Reconciliation as often as desired.

Frequent confession of venial sins is very beneficial. In a famous encyclical by Pius XII, we read: "It is true that venial sins may be expiated in many ways which are to be highly commended. But to ensure more rapid progress day by day in the path of virtue, we will that the pious practice of frequent confession, which was introduced into the Church by the inspiration of the Holy Spirit, should be earnestly advocated. By it genuine self-knowledge is increased, Christian humility grows, bad habits are corrected, spiritual neglect and tepidity are resisted, the conscience is purified, the will is strengthened, a salutary self-control is attained, and grace is increased in virtue of the sacrament itself" (The Mystical Body of Christ, no. 88).

Frequent confession of *venial* sins is desirable, but the confession of *mortal* sins is imperative. A mortal sin should be confessed soon.

What must we be careful of in frequent confessions?

In frequent confessions we must be careful to have true sorrow for sin and a real desire to correct ourselves. A sorrowless confession is invalid.

Contrition

What is contrition?

By contrition we mean true sorrow, which comes after one has offended God by sin. This sorrow has to come from love of God, fear of His punishments, or hatred of sin itself. By its very nature, this true sorrow implies that we detest our sins and resolve never to commit them again.

In the *Miserere*, David's prayer of repentance (Psalm 51), we can see the characteristics of sincere contrition.

Contrition must be:

1) interior—that is, genuine, not just an exterior show:

"My sacrifice, O God, is a contrite spirit;
   a heart contrite and humbled, O God, you will
      not spurn";

2) universal—extending to all the sins we have committed:

"Turn away your face from my sins,
   and blot out all my guilt";

3) supernatural—with motives based on faith:

"A clean heart create for me, O God,
   and a steadfast spirit renew within me";

4) supreme—with hatred for sin and willingness to suffer anything rather than to offend God again:

"For I acknowledge my offense,
   and my sin is before me always."

Is it possible to be sorry and yet not have perfect contrition?

There are two types of contrition: perfect and imperfect.

Perfect contrition is the result of one's hatred for sin because it offends God, whom we love above all things. It is founded on charity and is an implicit desire to receive the Sacrament of Reconciliation.

When speaking of Mary Magdalen, Jesus said, "I tell you, that is why her many sins are forgiven— because of her great love. Little is forgiven the one whose love is small" (Luke 7:47).

Imperfect contrition is called attrition. Sorrow is imperfect when we are sorry for our sins only because they are disgusting and hateful in themselves, or because we are afraid that God will punish us, or for some similar reason.

Is attrition sufficient for the reception of Penance?

Attrition is sufficient for the reception of Penance. However, there is another form of sorrow which has no supernatural motive at all (neither a hatred for sin because it is evil nor a fear of God's punishment). This purely natural sorrow (for having lost the esteem of others, for example) is not true contrition and has no value for the reception of Penance.

Is imperfect contrition, by itself, sufficient for the forgiveness of serious sins?

Imperfect contrition of itself, without the Sacrament of Reconciliation, cannot obtain pardon for serious sins.

More Questions
Frequently Asked

What is meant by the "seal of confession"?

By the seal of confession is meant the priest's obligation of secrecy. He must never reveal any matter heard in confession. No priest may break this seal even to save his own life.

Should we ever speak of what we have heard or said in confession?

With regard to overhearing someone else's confession, we are strictly bound to secrecy; regarding our own confession we are not. However, it is better not to talk about the advice given, the penance, etc.

What is the best age for first confession?

The new Code of Canon Law has reaffirmed that first confession should be made at the "age of reason" and before first Communion. The "age of reason" is regarded as seven or eight. At this time the child is moving from the instinctive phase of his development into the "second infancy"—the moral phase. This, noted the late Cardinal Wright, is "a very delicate and precise moment, an opportunity which cannot be missed without serious consequences for the future.... Without solicitous care from parents, priests and teachers, the instinctive life is prolonged through the 'second infancy' and beyond, with disastrous consequences on the spiritual destiny of the individual. To act in time to awaken the moral sense at the beginning of the age of discernment is to save the person at his roots."*

Where should confession take place?

Confession should take place in a confessional located in a church or chapel. Confessions are not to be heard outside the confessional without a just cause.

---

*John Cardinal Wright, *First Confession and First Communion*, St. Paul Editions.

What are the various ways in which the Sacrament of Penance is celebrated?

Penance is celebrated in three main ways:

—the reconciliation of individual penitents—individual confession and absolution;

—a communal celebration of the Word of God followed by individual confession and absolution;

—general absolution—which can be given only in certain exceptional instances, such as an imminent danger of death when there is not enough time for the priest or priests to hear individual confessions.

What should a penitent bear in mind when receiving general absolution?

As when receiving individual absolution, the penitent must bear in mind the necessity of being sorry, of making a resolution to avoid sin in the future, and of repairing any scandal or harm that he may have caused.

Does the recipient of a general absolution have any other obligations?

Once absolved, the penitent is free to receive Communion, for his sins have been forgiven. However, he has the obligation of telling these forgiven mortal sins in confession as soon as possible. Nor may he receive another general absolution until he has made this confession.

What is a penitential celebration?

A penitential celebration is a gathering of the faithful in which, for example, Scripture is read (with perhaps other readings as well), and a homily is preached, applying the biblical readings to life and conversion. Sacramental confession is not made, nor is absolution given. After the people have prayed together, they are dismissed by the leader of the assembly.

Such celebrations:

—foster the spirit of penance in the Christian community;
—help the faithful prepare for confession, which can be made individually or at a later time;
—help children gradually to form their consciences regarding sin in human life and freedom from sin through Christ;
—aid catechumens during their conversion;
—help penitents to attain perfect contrition in mission territories where no priest is available to give sacramental absolution.

John XXIII on Confession and God's Mercy

"St. Jean Marie Vianney...spent an average of fifteen hours a day in the confessional. This daily work started at one or two in the morning and did not end until nightfall. And when he collapsed of exhaustion, five days before his death, the last penitents gathered around the bed of the dying priest. It is estimated that toward the end of his life the yearly number of pilgrims to Ars had reached the figure of 80,000.

"It is difficult to imagine the physical discomfort, inconveniences and sufferings of these endless sessions in the confessional for a man already exhausted by fasts, privations, infirmity, and lack of rest and of sleep. But he was above all oppressed by moral pain. Listen to this lament of his: 'One offends the dear God so much that one might be tempted to invoke the end of the world.... One must come to Ars to know what sin is.... One does not know what to do. All one can do is to cry and pray.' The saint forgot to say that he also took upon himself a part of the expiation: 'As for me,' he confided to a person who came to him for advice, 'I assign a small penance to them and the rest I do myself for them.'

"And truly the Curé of Ars lived only for his 'poor sinners,' as he called them, in the hope of seeing them converted and repentant. Their conversion was the objective on which converged all his hopes and the work on which he spent all his time and all his efforts. And this because he knew from his experience of the confessional all the harm of sin and the frightful ruin wrought by it in the world of souls. He spoke of it in frightening terms: 'If we had faith and could see a soul in the state of mortal sin, we would die of fright.'

"But the bitterness of his sorrow and the vehemence of his words were due less to the fear of the eternal sorrows that threaten hardened sinners than to the emotion he felt at the thought of divine love ignored and offended. In the face of the sinner's obstinacy and his ungratefulness toward such a kind God, the tears would flow from his eyes. 'Oh, my friend,' he would say, 'I cry precisely because you do not cry.' But, on the other hand, with how much delicacy and how much fervor did he bring the rebirth of hope in penitent hearts. That is why he made himself the untiring minister of divine mercy, which is, he said, powerful, 'like the swirling torrent that carries away the hearts in its passage,' and more tender than the solicitude of a mother because God is 'more ready to forgive than would be a mother to retrieve one of her children from the fire'" (From the Beginning of Our Priesthood).

Anointing of the Sick

The Sacrament and Its Origin

What is the Anointing of the Sick?

The Anointing of the Sick is the sacrament by which Christ gives comfort and strength to the soul, and sometimes to the body, of a Catholic who is dangerously ill from sickness, injury, or old age.

How is the Anointing of the Sick given?

The Anointing of the Sick is given by the priest who anoints the sick person on the forehead and hands, saying the appropriate prayers.

What does this sacrament do for a person?

Through this sacrament, Christ:

—fortifies the sick person's soul with more grace and with the strength to resist temptations (for often temptations are strongest when one is physically weak);

—gives the sick person comfort to bear his sufferings bravely and courage and consolation in the face of death;

—cleanses the soul of venial sin;

—even removes mortal sin, if the person would have wished forgiveness but is unable to make his confession.

Sometimes the sacrament also restores physical health if that would be helpful for the sick person's salvation.

Where in Scripture do we find reference to the Anointing of the Sick?

In the Gospels, we find Jesus sending the disciples out to teach and to heal the sick:

"They went off, preaching the need of repentance. They expelled many demons, anointed the sick with oil, and worked many cures" (Mark 6:12-13).

This surely is a reference to the sacrament not present but to come.

On the other hand, in the letter of James, we find an outstanding passage:

"Is there anyone sick among you? He should ask for the presbyters of the church. They in turn are to pray over him, anointing him with oil in the Name [of the Lord.] This prayer uttered in faith will reclaim the one who is ill, and the Lord will restore him to health. If he has committed any sins, forgiveness will be his" (James 5:14-15).

The Minister and the Recipient

Can the Anointing of the Sick be validly administered by a lay person?

No. Only bishops and priests can validly administer the Anointing of the Sick.

When should a person receive Anointing of the Sick?

A person should receive the Anointing of the Sick when he *begins* to be in danger of death because of sickness, accident or old age. States Vatican II: "The Anointing of the Sick is not a sacrament for those only who are at the point of death. Hence, as soon as any one of the faithful begins to be in danger of death from sickness or old age, the fitting time for him to receive this sacrament has certainly already arrived" (Constitution on the Sacred Liturgy, no. 73). It is a good practice to ask a priest to visit sick members of one's family in the case of a serious illness, even though there is no apparent danger of death. Persons about to undergo surgery in connection with a dangerous illness should also be anointed. Sick children, too, may receive this sacrament if they are seriously ill and have attained the use of reason.

Can this sacrament be repeated?

Yes, this sacrament can be repeated in the event of another serious illness or a more serious crisis in the same sickness.

Can a priest anoint someone who is unconscious?

Yes. In fact, it is important that he do so. Through this sacrament even mortal sin will be removed from the soul if the unconscious person had at least imperfect contrition before losing consciousness.

When in doubt as to whether the sick person has reached the age of reason, or is dangerously ill, or is dead, should the sacrament be administered?

Yes, in any of these cases.

Preparation for the Sacrament

Where is the sacrament received?

This sacrament may be received in church, at home, in a hospital or—in the case of a serious accident—anywhere. At home, prepare a table in the sickroom, and cover it with a linen cloth. On it you may place, if possible, a crucifix, two candles, and some holy water.

What is necessary in order to receive this sacrament worthily?

The Anointing of the Sick cannot be worthily received if the sick person is in a state of mortal sin and is capable of going to confession. In other words, if the person can confess his serious sins he is obliged to do so before being anointed. (If, however, he is unconscious, the anointing will remove even mortal sins under the conditions we have cited.)

Are there other dispositions which the sick person should cultivate?

Faith in Christ's saving passion and death, faith in everlasting life, and a willingness to offer oneself to God together with the suffering Christ—all these are dispositions which the Church encourages in one who is to receive the Anointing of the Sick. States Vatican II:

"By the sacred Anointing of the Sick and the prayer of her priests the whole Church commends the sick to the suffering and glorified Lord, asking that He may lighten their suffering and save them; she exhorts them, moreover, to contribute to the welfare of the whole People of God by associating themselves freely with the passion and death of Christ" (Dogmatic Constitution on the Church, no. 11).

Sickness and the Anointing in the Mystery of Salvation

"Sickness and pain have always been a heavy burden for man and an enigma to his understanding. Christians suffer sickness and pain as do all other men; yet their faith helps them to understand better the mystery of suffering and to bear their pain more bravely. From Christ's words they know that sickness has meaning and value for their own salvation and for the world's; they also know that Christ loved the sick and that during His life He often looked upon the sick and healed them.

"Sickness, while it is closely related to man's sinful condition, cannot be considered a punishment which man suffers for his personal sins (see John 9:3). Christ Himself was sinless, yet He fulfilled what was written in Isaiah: He bore all the sufferings of His pas-

sion and understood human sorrow (see Isaiah 53:4-5).
Christ still suffers and is tormented in His followers
whenever we suffer. If we realize that our sufferings
are preparing us for eternal life in glory, then they will
seem short and even easy to bear (see 2 Corinthians
4:17)....

"The sacrament of anointing prolongs the concern which the Lord Himself showed for the bodily
and spiritual welfare of the sick, as the Gospels testify,
and which He asked His followers to show also. This
sacrament has its beginning in Christ and is spoken of
in the letter of James: the Church, by the Anointing
of the Sick and the prayer of the priest, commends
those who are ill to the suffering and glorified Lord,
that He may raise them up and save them (see James
5:14-16). Moreover, the Church exhorts them to contribute to the welfare of the People of God by associating themselves freely with the passion and death of
Christ (see Romans 8:17). The man who is seriously ill
needs the special help of God's grace in this time of
anxiety, lest he be broken in spirit and subject to temptations and the weakening of faith.

"Christ, therefore, strengthens the faithful who
are afflicted by illness with the sacrament of anointing, providing them with the strongest means of
support.

"The celebration of this sacrament consists especially in the laying on of hands by the presbyters of the
Church, their offering the prayer of faith, and the
anointing of the sick with oil made holy by God's blessing. This rite signifies the grace of the sacrament and
confers it.

"This sacrament provides the sick person with the
grace of the Holy Spirit by which the whole man is
brought to health, trust in God is encouraged, and
strength is given to resist the temptations of the Evil

One and anxiety about death. Thus the sick person is able not only to bear his suffering bravely, but also to fight against it. A return to physical health may even follow the reception of this sacrament if it will be beneficial to the sick person's salvation. If necessary, the sacrament also provides the sick person with the forgiveness of sins and the completion of Christian penance.

"The Anointing of the Sick, which includes the prayer of faith (see James 5:15), is a sacrament of faith. This faith is important for the minister and particularly for the one who receives it. The sick man will be saved by his faith and the faith of the Church which looks back to the death and resurrection of Christ, the source of the sacrament's power (see James 5:15), and looks ahead to the future kingdom which is pledged in the sacraments" (Introduction to the Rite of the Anointing of the Sick, nos. 1, 2, 5-7).

Holy Orders

The Sacrament and Its Origin

What is Holy Orders?
Holy Orders is the sacrament through which men are given the grace and power to carry out the sacred duties of deacons, priests or bishops, feeding the faithful with the Word and the grace of God.

What does the term "Orders" refer to?
The term "Orders" refers to the various levels of the Catholic ministry. There are three degrees of ordination: to the diaconate, to the priesthood, to the episcopate. In other words, the Church's ordained ministers are deacons, priests and bishops.

When was this sacrament instituted?
Christ instituted this sacrament at the Last Supper when He gave the Apostles and their successors the power to offer Mass: "Do this as a remembrance of me" (Luke 22:19).

On the day of His resurrection Christ gave His Apostles the second great power of the priest, that of forgiving sins.

Just before His ascension, our Lord gave His disciples the mandate to preach the Gospel and administer the sacraments.

"Full authority has been given to me
both in heaven and on earth;

go, therefore, and make disciples of all the nations.
Baptize them in the name
'of the Father,
and of the Son,
and of the Holy Spirit.'
Teach them to carry out everything I have commanded
    you.
And know that I am with you always, until the end of
    the world" (Matthew 28:18-20).

Holy Orders is continued by succession. Jesus knew that His Apostles were to die, and He provided for the passing on of their power. The Apostles understood the Lord's intention and ordained worthy men to continue their apostolic office: "I remind you to stir into flame the gift of God bestowed when my hands were laid on you," St. Paul wrote to Timothy (2 Timothy 1:6).

The Minister and the Recipient

Who is the minister of this sacrament?
    The bishop, who acts as a successor of the Apostles, is the minister of Holy Orders.

Who may receive the Sacrament of Holy Orders?
    Only an unmarried Catholic man is potentially eligible for the priesthood in the Latin rite.
    Permanent deacons in the Latin rite may be married if they were so before their ordination; however, after ordination to the diaconate a deacon may not marry (or remarry if his wife has died).
    In the Eastern rites, ordination to the priesthood can be conferred on married men with the same conditions as ordination to the permanent diaconate in the West.

Why is it that the Church does not ordain women?

The Church follows the example of Christ, who did not ordain even His own Mother. Christianity did much to raise the status of women in the early centuries of the Church, yet never were there women priests—even though pagan cults did have priestesses. This shows an awareness among the early Christians that Christ intended that only men should be ordained. And, when one considers that the priest acts "in the person of Christ," who became a man, the bestowal of the priesthood only on men seems fitting. We must keep in mind that the priesthood is not a *right;* it is a *gift* of God—a gift not so much to the individual but to the Church. One's potential can be fulfilled without priestly ordination.

Ordination and Its Effects

How is a man ordained a priest?

Priestly ordination is given through the bishop's laying on of hands, followed by a special prayer, asking God to give these men the dignity of the priesthood. From that moment on they are priests.

What does the laying on of hands stand for?

Placing one's hands, palms downward, on another person's head stands for the conferring of the grace and power of the Holy Spirit.

What are the chief effects of priestly ordination?

In becoming a priest a man receives the power to change bread and wine into Christ's Body and Blood. He also receives the power to forgive sins in Christ's name and to administer the Anointing of the Sick. His soul receives the spiritual seal ("character") of a priest and a greater share in God's life—grace.

Questions Frequently Asked

What is the difference between diocesan priests and religious priests?

Diocesan priests are directly under the bishop. At ordination they promise obedience to the bishop and to his successors. They also make a commitment to celibacy. Religious priests are members of religious congregations or orders. They profess the vows of poverty, chastity and obedience and are subject in various ways to the bishop and the Holy Father through their religious superiors.

Why is celibacy required of priests in the Latin rite?

The Church in the West made celibacy obligatory centuries ago. By living a celibate life the priest is free from marital concerns and duties which could hamper his total dedication to God and to His people. In his celibate life the priest seeks to imitate Christ, who never married and who taught by word and example the superior excellence of celibacy lived for the sake of the kingdom of heaven.

What are the chief powers given in the ordination of bishops?

In ordination to the episcopate ("episcopal consecration"), the fullness of the priesthood is conferred. A bishop has the power to ordain priests and to confirm. He is a successor of the Apostles. Often, powers of jurisdiction over a diocese are received by a bishop when he is ordained. These powers to administer a diocese and serve its faithful as their shepherd and chief teacher are not conveyed automatically by the Sacrament of Orders itself but rather are granted the right of exercise by the Pope, who has called this priest to the episcopacy. (In the same way, priests receive powers of jurisdiction from their bishops—but priests exercise these powers, so to say, in the bishop's name, whereas a bishop exercises his powers in his *own* name, as a successor of the Apostles.) In union with the Pope and under him, bishops are able to make infallible pronouncements in ecumenical councils. Since 1967, the bishops of the world have been meeting regularly in Rome in representative meetings called synods to advise the Holy Father on important questions concerning the whole Church.

Who is the Pope?

The Pope is the Bishop of Rome, the Successor of St. Peter, whom Christ made the visible head of the Church. As the Vicar of Christ, the Pope teaches, shepherds and sanctifies the entire Church. The Holy Spirit assists the Pope in a special way, so that his solemn pronouncements (definitions) on faith and morals for the whole Church are infallibly true.

Are bishops ordained by the Pope?

Bishops *may be* ordained by the Pope, but normally other bishops perform the rite.

What is the meaning of such titles as "monsignor," "archbishop," and "cardinal"?

"Monsignor" is a title of honor given to a priest in recognition for services rendered to the Church. An archbishop is usually the bishop of a larger diocese, called an archdiocese. A cardinal is a bishop who has been chosen to be a special adviser of the Pope. Some cardinals are engaged full-time at the Vatican, taking care of the affairs of the universal Church. Others administer their own dioceses but keep in close contact with the Holy See. In the event of a Pope's death, the cardinals meet in a secret assembly called a conclave to elect his Successor.

What is the role of deacons in the Church?

Deacons are ordained to help bishops and priests by carrying out such ministries as: preaching, baptizing, distributing Holy Communion, giving Eucharistic benediction, reading the Scriptures to the faithful, and blessing couples who are receiving Matrimony.

Is it important to promote vocations to the priesthood?

It is very important to promote vocations to the priesthood. Today especially, the Church has a great need for generous young men to feed the faithful the bread of God's Word and the bread of Christ's Body, to absolve them of their sins and bring them strength and comfort in time of illness. Without the priesthood, there could be no Church.

A young man who feels called by God and who has been accepted as a candidate for the priesthood should do all in his power to persevere, realizing that he has been specially chosen to assume the awesome dignity of *alter Christus*—"another Christ"—God's representative among men.

He Who Hears Them Hears Christ

"Bishops...with their helpers, the priests and deacons, have taken up the service of the community, presiding in place of God over the flock, whose shepherds they are, as teachers for doctrine, priests for sacred worship, and ministers for governing. And just as the office granted individually to Peter, the first among the Apostles, is permanent and is to be transmitted to his Successors, so also the Apostles' office of nurturing the Church is permanent, and is to be exercised without interruption by the sacred order of bishops. Therefore, the Sacred Council teaches that bishops by divine institution have succeeded to the place of the Apostles, as shepherds of the Church, and he who hears them, hears Christ, and he who rejects them, rejects Christ and Him who sent Christ" (Dogmatic Constitution on the Church, no. 20).

Matrimony

The Sacrament and Its Origin

What is marriage?

Marriage is the unbreakable union of man and woman. For non-Christians, it is the noblest of natural contracts; for Christians it is a sacrament—a sacred sign through which Christ gives His grace. This sacrament is also called Matrimony.

What is Matrimony?

Matrimony is the sacrament through which a baptized man and a baptized woman join themselves for life in a lawful marriage and receive God's grace so that they may carry out their responsibilities.

Why is marriage sometimes spoken of as a covenant?

Marriage is sometimes called a covenant because it is a lifelong commitment. St. Paul tells us that Christian marriage is a sacred sign that reflects the lasting covenant which unites Christ to His Church.

What is the purpose of marriage?

The purpose of marriage is twofold: unity and procreation, or the giving of love and the giving of life. The spouses commit themselves to loving, lifelong service—to one another and to the children whom God will send them.

Vatican II teaches: "Marriage and conjugal love are by their nature ordained toward the begetting and educating of children. Children are really the supreme gift of marriage and contribute very substantially to the welfare of their parents....

"Marriage to be sure is not instituted solely for procreation. Rather, its very nature as an unbreakable compact between persons, and the welfare of the children, both demand that the mutual love of the spouses be embodied in a rightly ordered manner, that it grow and ripen" (Constitution on the Church in the Modern World, no. 50).

When we speak of *Christian* marriage, another dimension must also be included: growth in holiness. The spouses help one another to become holier; moreover, children and parents reciprocally contribute to the sanctification of one another.

Why is marriage a sacrament?

Marriage is a sacrament because Jesus Christ chose to raise it to this level. As with three other sacraments, we do not know the precise occasion of institution, but both Scripture and Tradition manifest the sacramental nature of marriage.

For example, in St. Paul's letter to the Ephesians (5:21-31), the Apostle compares Christian marriage to the permanent union of Christ and the Church. In this comparison St. Paul intimates that just as the union between Christ and His Church is a supernatural union which produces grace, so does the union produced by Matrimony confer grace on the husband and wife. So, he intimates that it is a sacrament, a grace-giving sign.

Another scriptural proof of the institution of Matrimony by Christ is His own emphasis on the permanence of marriage: "Therefore, let no man separate what God has joined" (Matthew 19:6). When the disciples heard this, they were amazed at their Master's difficult teaching, and from their surprise we can infer both that special grace from God is necessary to preserve the marriage union and that Jesus would never have taught such a demanding doctrine without instituting the Sacrament of Matrimony to provide us with all the necessary graces.

Finally, early Christian writings speak of marriage as something supernatural which of itself confers grace on the man and woman who receive it, and the Council of Trent formally defined that Matrimony is one of the seven sacraments.

How is the Sacrament of Matrimony conferred?

Matrimony is conferred when a baptized man and a baptized woman express their mutual consent under conditions established or permitted by the Church. The bride and groom, therefore, confer the sacrament on one another.

In a mixed marriage, do the spouses receive the sacrament?

A mixed marriage is a valid, sacramental marriage for both spouses, if both have been validly baptized, have obtained the proper dispensation, and marry according to the other norms established by the Church. If one of the parties is not baptized, but the other necessary conditions (dispensation, etc.) have been fulfilled, the Catholic party—according to the opinion of some theologians—does receive the sacrament, but today most theologians would deny this. The non-Catholic, of course, could not, because Baptism is a prerequisite to all the other sacraments.

Could it happen that one might go through the marriage ceremony according to the Church's norms, yet not be truly married?

This does happen, and therefore the Church sometimes grants decrees of nullity (annulments). A decree of nullity is decision by a marriage tribunal that an apparently valid marriage was actually invalid from the beginning. If, for example, the spouses had been pressured into the marriage by their parents because a child was on the way, that marriage would be invalid. The consent of Matrimony must be free, not forced. The marriage would also be invalid if one or both of the spouses married with the intention of never having children, or of breaking up the marriage if all did not go smoothly. Marriage must be undertaken as a free, irrevocable, lifelong commitment to one's spouse and to the children God may send.

The Effects of Matrimony

What are the effects of the Sacrament of Matrimony?

The effects of the sacrament are: 1) an invisible bond that will last until the death of one of the spouses; and 2) the graces of the sacrament.

What are the special graces of the Sacrament of Matrimony?

When received in the state of grace, Matrimony increases sanctifying grace in the souls of the spouses. Every sacrament also gives to the recipient its own special grace, called sacramental grace. In Matrimony the sacramental grace brings to the couple the assurance of God's help to persevere together and grow in love, fidelity and holiness. Marriage is for life, and God, who in His great wisdom knows the weakness of human nature (which, in spite of goodwill, can cause friction in the best of marriages), provides through sacramental grace a constant source of strength for the couple. The sacramental grace of Matrimony includes the right to all the graces which are necessary to preserve mutual love in spite of anything and everything; the graces to face and overcome all difficulties, misunderstandings, sicknesses, or worries. The promise of graces which a couple receives in Matrimony does not last only for a year or two, but for an entire lifetime.

Anyone thinking of the great responsibilities of marriage and of the unforeseeable difficulties the future could hold might hesitate to enter into marriage. However, we must never forget God's role in the couple's life and His constant and infallible help, which is such an important and consoling aspect of the Sacrament of Matrimony.

Are these graces of special importance today?

These graces are especially important today because there are many pressures and harmful influences in our society which make married life difficult and attempt to downgrade the importance of a strong family life.

Might one receive Matrimony without receiving all the effects?

Yes. It could happen that a person receive the sacrament in a state of mortal sin. This would be a sacrilege, but the bond of Matrimony would be established nonetheless. With the restoration of grace (normally, through the Sacrament of Penance), the graces of Matrimony would also be received.

The Responsibilities of the Married

What are the chief duties of spouses to one another?

The chief duties of the spouses to one another are: 1) fidelity; 2) cohabitation; and 3) mutual assistance. Fidelity means that each partner in a marriage is bound to refrain from any activity proper only to marriage with any person other than the spouse. Cohabitation is a principle of the natural law which teaches that a husband and wife should live together and may separate temporarily and with mutual consent only for sufficiently important reasons, such as a temporary job transfer, etc. Mutual assistance includes mutual love and friendship and cooperation in regard to the financial support of the family. The normal way in which spouses help one another in the managing of the home is for the husband to work in order to receive a salary and the wife to take charge of household affairs and the care of the children, perhaps also supplementing the husband's income by holding a part-time job.

What are the duties of parents toward their children?

The duties of a mother to her child begin as soon as she realizes she is pregnant, even if she is not absolutely certain, because at this time she must begin to abstain from anything that might injure the fetus—such as heavy work or strenuous exercise and the improper use of drugs and alcohol.

Once the child has been born, the parents have a grave obligation to have him baptized as soon as possible. From the time of the baby's birth to the point at which he is able to provide for himself, the parents have the obligation to provide for their child's physical, intellectual and spiritual needs. Providing for the physical needs of children includes giving them the proper and necessary food, clothing and shelter. Parents have the duty to see to it that their children receive all the necessary education, remembering that while formal education is useful and needed, the first real school is the family itself.

Important for the emotional growth of the children is the parents' avoidance of favoritism or the making of harmful comparisons.

Spiritual training of their children is also a duty of parents, who have the obligation to raise their offspring in such a way that their lives are directed always toward God, their Creator. Such spiritual training must include instructions on the truths of faith and morals, supervision and help in fulfilling religious and moral obligations, good advice and especially good example. Parents should send their children to Catholic schools whenever possible, and when this cannot be done they must provide adequate religious instruction for the children outside of school. Normally this will include regular attendance at parish CCD classes.

Are Catholic couples obliged to have as many children as possible?

No, Catholic couples are obliged only to act in a truly responsible manner in bringing children into the world and raising them well. This responsibility includes the recognition of the procreation of children as one of the fundamental purposes of marriage, and the avoidance of abortion and artificial birth control as contrary to God's law.

Why are abortion and the use of artificial means of birth control seriously sinful?

Abortion and contraception are seriously sinful because they are against both the natural and divine law. Artificial birth control is evil because it frustrates the natural activity of the body which God has ordained for the procreation of children. Direct abortion, the intentional killing of the fetus, is murder and cannot be permitted.

What is indirect abortion?

Indirect abortion occurs when the fetus dies as a result of an operation performed on the mother. Indirect abortion is not sinful if the death of the fetus was not intended, but only tolerated out of necessity in order to save at least the life of the mother. Such an operation resulting in the death of the fetus is permitted only when it is certain that without the operation both mother and child would die. The fetus must always be baptized.

Is there an acceptable method of birth control?

The Church recognizes natural methods of birth control (as opposed to artificial), because these do not directly block God's creative action. (Information about natural methods may be obtained from the addresses at the back of this book.)

Is a marriage rendered invalid by childlessness?

A truly valid marriage is not rendered invalid by circumstances that develop later. Therefore, if a couple married with the intention of accepting the children God would send them, childlessness would not render their marriage invalid. Vatican II teaches: "Marriage persists as a whole manner and communion of life, and maintains its value and indissolubility, even when, despite the often intense desire of the couple, offspring are lacking" (Constitution on the Church in the Modern World, no. 50).

What are the chief characteristics of marriage?

The chief characteristics of marriage are unity and indissolubility. These characteristics apply to *all* marriages, whether sacramental or not. They are rooted in the law of God. Marriage must join one man and one woman for life.

Fallen human nature is weak in this regard. In fact, even God's chosen people were permitted to relax their standards. The Sacrament of Matrimony was instituted to help couples maintain the unity and fidelity which the divine law imposes. Jesus explained that He was reestablishing the original order willed by God:

Then some Pharisees came up and as a test began to ask him whether it was permissible for a husband to divorce his wife. In reply he said, "What command did Moses give you?" They answered, "Moses permitted divorce and the writing of a decree of divorce." But Jesus told them: "He wrote that commandment for you because of your stubbornness. At the beginning of creation God made them male and female; for this reason a man shall leave his father and mother and the two shall become as one. They are no longer two but one flesh. Therefore let no man separate what God has joined." Back in the house again, the disciples began to question him about this. He told them, "Whoever divorces his wife and marries another commits adultery against her; and the woman who divorces her husband and marries another commits adultery" (Mark 10:2-12).

Is the indissolubility of marriage beneficial?

Definitely. Among the advantages of this unbreakable oneness are: the security that husband and wife enjoy; mutual fidelity and mutual help; domestic and social peace and order; the procreation of children and their good upbringing.

Is divorce ever permissible?

If by "divorce" we mean the dissolving of a valid marriage, this can almost never be done.* Normally the marriage bond is dissolved only by the death of one of the spouses.

But if by "divorce" we mean the civil process by which the *state* "dissolves" a marriage, the Church does permit such a procedure when a couple has a serious reason for separating. Neither of the spouses is free to remarry, however, for in the eyes of God and of the Church they have only separated; they are still married to one another.

---

*There are two rare cases in which the Church allows a valid marriage to be dissolved. The first is the "Pauline privilege." This teaching is based on 1 Corinthians 7:12-17 and concerns the relation-

What are some reasons for the Church to grant permission to separate?

The reason for *perpetual* separation arises from adultery of one of the partners. Other causes which permit the injured partner to seek a *temporary or indefinite* separation are: criminal or shameful conduct, the education of the children in schism or heresy, grave danger to soul and body. A priest should be consulted normally.

Did Jesus make an exception to the law of indissolubility?

In Matthew 19:9, we find the so-called *porneia* clause, which has been variously translated—"except for unchastity" (RSV), "lewd conduct is a separate case" (NAB), "I am not speaking of fornication" (JB)— and also variously understood. Whatever the phrase's meaning, however, theologians are agreed that Jesus was not making an exception. In the parallel passages —Mark 10:11ff., and Luke 16:18—we find no exception. Another source to be consulted is 1 Corinthians 7:10-11.

Scripture is a harmonious whole and does not contradict itself. Hence the *porneia* clause has to be regarded as in accord with the rest of the New Testament teaching.

---

ship between two unbaptized persons who have married and even consummated their marriage. If one of these spouses is later baptized, and the other spouse is opposed to Christianity and no longer consents to live with the Christian spouse or poses a threat to the Christian's faith or moral life, the marriage may be dissolved. The Christian spouse is then free to remarry. The second case in which a marriage may be dissolved is when a marriage between baptized persons or between a baptized person and one not baptized has not been consummated by the marriage act. For serious reasons and under certain conditions such a non-consummated marriage may be dissolved by a dispensation from the Holy Father or by the profession of solemn vows in a religious order of one of the persons.

Is a climate of divorce harmful to Christian marriage?

Such a climate is very harmful. The ease with which a man or woman can obtain a civil divorce constitutes an ever-present threat which fosters insecurity, instability, infidelity and the limitation of offspring. When a civil divorce has actually been obtained, the children suffer, torn between conflicting loyalties, and are neglected and even rejected. Their unhappiness, in turn, fosters alcoholism, drug addiction, crime and other social disorders. A society which permits easy divorce is tending towards its own destruction.

What are some needs of today's divorced Catholic?

Today's divorced Catholic needs:

—special guidance not to become bitter, not to talk about "rules of the Church," when these are the rules of Christ;

—guidance in keeping with the eternal teachings of Christ to overcome feelings of loneliness and desolation;

—encouragement to keep close to the sacraments, especially Holy Communion;

—encouragement never to enter into an invalid marriage, because this cuts one off from receiving the life-giving and life-sustaining sacraments.

What is recommended for a Catholic living in an invalid marriage?

For a Catholic living in an invalid marriage, the religious problems are greater and the need for counseling is also greater. Such Catholics must never lose hope or lose sight of salvation. They should by all means remain faithful to Sunday Mass, parish life and personal prayer. It is a difficult way to live and reach salvation—but the mercy of God is great, especially to the contrite of heart.

Preparation for Matrimony

Does everyone have a right to marry?

The Church has always considered marriage as a natural right. However, she wisely asks that Catholics not exercise this right until they have reached sufficient psychological maturity. In our time and culture such maturity is generally not achieved until young persons have entered their twenties.

What does psychological maturity involve?

Such maturity involves an *understanding* that marriage is a lifelong, total commitment between a man and woman ordered to mutual love and help and the procreation and education of children, coupled with a realistic *awareness* of the types of difficulties to be encountered and the means of coping with them. It also involves *freedom and firmness of will*—freedom from outside pressures and true willingness to commit oneself to a life of loving service.

A person is psychologically *immature* if he repeatedly wavers in his opinions and convictions, is childish in his attitudes and viewpoints, and lacks emotional control. Someone who shows such immaturity should be advised to seek help in growing toward maturity before facing the serious commitment of marriage.

How do we know that people are free to marry?

The Episcopal Conference determines what inquiries should be made to determine that nothing stands in the way of true marriage.

What are some of the major impediments to Christian marriage?

The most serious impediments are called diriment impediments, and they make an attempted marriage invalid, unless (when possible) a dispensation is obtained. In other words, if a couple were to go through with a marriage ceremony in spite of these obstacles there would be no marriage.

Some diriment impediments are: lack of age (a boy must be at least sixteen and a girl fourteen); close blood relationship, as between relatives closer than second cousins; antecedent and perpetual impotence for intercourse, on the part of either the man or the woman; the bond of a previous marriage; difference of worship (one party is not baptized); clerical state (one party is a priest or deacon); a perpetual religious vow of chastity binding one or both parties.

A lesser impediment, which may be dispensed from by the local ordinary, is the difference of worship between members of two Christian confessions. In other words, the Church does not encourage the so-called "mixed marriages," but a diocesan bishop may grant permission for such a marriage if the reasons presented by the prospective spouses seem sufficient.

What should preparation for Christian marriage include?

A couple preparing for Matrimony should pray for God's help and direction and study the beauty, nobility and duties of the married life. They should practice virtue, especially chastity, and ask the advice of those who can be of great help to them, particularly their parents and the priest to whom they usually go to confession. Frequent reception of the Sacraments of

Penance and Holy Eucharist will also bring the grace which is needed to prepare for and begin their married life. The couple should also attend the Pre-Cana or similar courses offered by their diocese, which provide valuable helps and instruction in preparation for the sacrament.

What is necessary for the worthy reception of Matrimony?

To receive the sacrament worthily, it is necessary to be in the state of grace (that is, free from mortal sin), to know and understand the duties of married life, and to obey the laws of the Church concerning marriage.

How does the marriage of a Catholic take place?

To be valid the marriage of a Catholic—whether to another Catholic or to a non-Catholic—is to take place in the presence of the local ordinary or the pastor (or a priest or deacon delegated by either of them) and two witnesses.* The sacrament is conferred by each spouse on the other when they express their mutual consent to the marriage, promising lifelong fidelity. These promises may be stated by the spouses (there are two formulas approved for use in the United States), or else the bride and groom may individually respond "I do" to the questions asked by the person officiating.

---

*For sufficiently weighty reasons, the Church may grant a dispensation allowing a Catholic to be married before a non-Catholic minister or even a civil official. Also, when no priest or deacon will be available for a month (as in mission territories) a man and woman may marry in the presence of two witnesses and then have the marriage registered in Church records. When someone is at the point of death, and no competent priest is available, he or she may marry before two witnesses. (This might be done, for example, to rectify a common-law marriage, if neither spouse was bound by a previous marriage bond.)

What is the role of the state concerning Matrimony?

Marriage is by its nature a social institution, and so it is necessary that it come under the authority of society's laws. Marriages of the unbaptized are in fact entirely under the authority of the state, because the state has power to govern in areas where only the natural law is concerned. However, the case of Christian marriage is different, because by the positive and divine law of Jesus, all marriages involving two baptized persons (or a baptized person and a non-baptized person) are subject to the jurisdiction of the Catholic Church. As a consequence, civil laws which interfere with the sacramental nature of marriage and its essential properties (such as laws permitting divorce or abortion) are evil and unjust. However, all civil laws relating to marriage which do not violate the Christian conscience should be obeyed, and no sacramental marriage should be entered into without also fulfilling all the civil requirements for marriage established by the state.

Mixed Marriages

What is a mixed marriage?

A mixed marriage is a marriage between a Catholic and (strictly speaking) a baptized non-Catholic.

Why does the Church urge Catholics to contract marriage only with Catholics?

The union of husband and wife in Matrimony is a sign of Christ's union with the Church. Married partners are called to perfect union of mind and communion of life, and this union can be broken or weakened when differences of opinion or disagreement touch on matters of religious truths and convictions. Religion is such a vital force that when a couple cannot share it, they feel something missing from their union. The greater the difference in religious beliefs, the greater the potential for problems.

What other facts should be known by a couple contemplating a mixed marriage?

The Catholic spouse must declare that he or she is ready to remove all dangers to his or her faith. He or she also has the grave obligation to promise to do all possible to have each of the children baptized and raised as a Catholic.

At an opportune time, the non-Catholic partner must be told about the promise which the Catholic spouse must make, so that the non-Catholic is fully aware of his or her partner's obligations before the actual marriage.

Both partners are to be well instructed regarding the purpose and essential properties of Christian marriage.

A Catholic priest (or deacon) and a non-Catholic minister may not officiate together at a mixed marriage, each performing his respective rite. The Church also forbids that another religious ceremony be held either before or after the Catholic ceremony.

A Catholic and an Orthodox marry validly if any sacred minister is present; for such a marriage to be lawful, however, two dispensations are necessary— one from the impediment of mixed religion and the other from the obligation of marrying before a priest (or deacon) and two witnesses.

Bishops and parish priests should have special care for the spiritual welfare of the Catholic spouse and the children of a mixed marriage, and should foster unity between the husband and wife.

The Family—
School of Humanity and Holiness

"Christian spouses, in virtue of the Sacrament of Matrimony, whereby they signify and partake of the mystery of that unity and fruitful love which exists between Christ and His Church, help each other to attain to holiness in their married life and in the rearing and education of their children. By reason of their state and rank in life they have their own special gift among the People of God. From the wedlock of Christians there comes the family, in which new citizens of human society are born, who by the grace of the Holy Spirit received in Baptism are made children of God, thus perpetuating the People of God through the centuries. The family is, so to speak, the domestic Church. In it parents should, by their word and example, be the first preachers of the Faith to their children; they should encourage them in the vocation which is proper to each of them, fostering with special care vocation to a sacred state" (Dogmatic Constitution on the Church, no. 11).

Sacramentals

Sacramentals in General

What are sacramentals?

Sacramentals are holy things or actions with which the Church asks God to grant us favors, especially spiritual ones.

Is there any biblical evidence for the use of sacramentals?

Scripture speaks of how God told the chosen people to use material things such as ashes, water, and even graven images in the Old Law (see Numbers 19:1-22; 21:4-9; John 3:14-15).

Christ Himself used gestures and ceremonies: blessings, laying on of hands, etc. The early Christians obviously believed that God's blessing could be attached to inanimate objects: "God worked extraordinary miracles at the hands of Paul. When handkerchiefs or cloths which had touched his skin were applied to the sick, their diseases were cured and evil spirits departed from them" (Acts 19:11-12). And in writing to Timothy, Paul speaks of things that have been "made holy by God's word and by prayer" (1 Timothy 4:5).

Do sacramentals obtain blessings and favors from God?

Sacramentals do obtain favors from God through the prayers of God's people offered for those who make use of them, and because of the devotion they inspire.

How are sacramentals different from sacraments?

Sacramentals differ from sacraments in this manner: the sacraments *give* grace directly through the actions of Jesus, while sacramentals help us indirectly to obtain God's grace.

Generally speaking, our own dispositions of faith and devotion are quite important in our use of sacramentals. However, there is one type of sacramental that infallibly produces its effect: the blessing that consecrates a person or thing to the service of God.

What are some kinds of sacramentals?

The sacramentals include:
—the ceremonies associated with the sacraments that are not part of the sacramental sign itself
—exorcisms for the removal of evil spirits
—blessings
—consecrations
—the use of blessed or consecrated objects
—the blessed or consecrated objects themselves.

Particular Sacramentals

What are blessings?

Blessings are words and actions by which a thing or person is placed under the care of God.

Which blessed objects of devotion are most commonly used among Catholics?

Blessed objects of devotion most commonly used among Catholics are rosaries; relics; medals; crucifixes; scapulars; pictures of Jesus, Mary, the saints; ashes; palms; candles.

Do blessed objects bring good luck?

Sacramentals should never be considered good luck charms, nor made the objects of superstition. For example, one cannot lead an immoral life because he believes that the scapular or medal he wears will grant him the grace of conversion before he dies.

What is a scapular?

A scapular consists of two small pieces of cloth, fastened by strings and worn around the neck in front and in back. The most common scapular honors Mary as our Lady of Mount Carmel. A scapular medal may be worn in place of a scapular.

What is holy water?

Holy water is water blessed by a priest in order to give God's blessing to those who use it.

Why do we make the Sign of the Cross with holy water upon entering and leaving church?

We make the Sign of the Cross with holy water upon entering and leaving church to remind ourselves of our baptismal commitment and promises.

What is the purpose of blessed candles?

Blessed candles are lit to witness to our devotion to Jesus, who is light and life with His grace.

What is the purpose of blessed ashes?

Blessed ashes are used especially on Ash Wednesday, the first day of Lent. A cross is traced with ashes on our forehead as a reminder to live a good life and do penance because one day we will die and return to dust.

What is the purpose of crucifixes, medals, scapulars, religious statues and holy pictures?

Crucifixes, medals, scapulars, religious statues and holy pictures serve as reminders of our holy Faith, heaven, etc.

Do we pray to religious statues and pictures?

We do not pray *to* the religious statues and pictures themselves. Instead, we pray to the person in heaven whom the statue or picture represents.

What is the purpose of the rosary beads?

The rosary beads are "prayer beads" which, when blessed, are enriched with many indulgences for reciting the prescribed prayers. These beads are used to recite the "Gospel prayer" made up of Our Father's, Hail Mary's and Glory's, in which we think about important events in the lives of Jesus and Mary.

The Importance of Sacramentals

"For well-disposed members of the faithful, the liturgy of the sacraments and sacramentals sanctifies almost every event in their lives; they are given access to the stream of divine grace which flows from the Paschal Mystery of the passion, death and resurrection of Christ, the font from which all sacraments and sacramentals draw their power. There is hardly a proper use of material things which cannot thus be directed toward the sanctification of men and the praise of God" (Constitution on the Sacred Liturgy, no. 61).

The Liturgy of the Hours

What is the Liturgy of the Hours?

The Liturgy of the Hours is a form of prayer in which God speaks to His people and the Church praises Him in song, interceding for the salvation of the world.

This form of prayer is not only for priests, seminarians and religious. Other members of the Christian faithful are also invited to take part in the Liturgy of the Hours, for it is the action of the whole Church.

Appendix I

Basic Truths

Compiled from the documents of Vatican II, post-conciliar documents, and other approved sources.

Our Living God

God, the beginning and end of all things, can be known with certainty from created reality by the light of human reason.

God's existence can also be known from supernatural revelation.

There is only one God.
God is absolutely unchangeable.
God is eternal.
God is almighty.
God is infinitely just.
God is infinitely merciful.

In God there are three Persons, the Father, the Son and the Holy Spirit. Each of the three Persons possesses the one divine Essence.

God's Care for His World

All that exists outside God was produced out of nothing by God.

God was moved by His goodness to create the world.

God keeps all created things in existence.

God, through His Providence, protects and guides all that He has created.

Man and His God

The first man was created by God.

Man consists of two essential parts—a material body and a spiritual soul.

God has conferred on man a supernatural destiny. There can be neither justice nor peace in the world, so long as men fail to realize how great is their dignity; for they have been created by God and are His children.

Man has in his heart a law written by God; to obey it is the very dignity of man; according to it he will be judged.

Our first parents, before the fall, were endowed with sanctifying grace, which is a sharing in God's divine life.

Our first parents in paradise sinned grievously through transgression of a divine command.

Through sin our first parents lost sanctifying grace.

Our first parents became subject to death and to the dominion of the devil.

Adam's sin is transmitted to his descendants, not by imitation, but by descent.

In the state of original sin man is deprived of sanctifying grace. Affected by original sin, men have frequently fallen into many errors concerning the true God, the nature of man, and the principles of the moral law.

In the design of God, every man is called upon to develop and fulfill himself, for every life is a vocation.

At birth, everyone is granted, in germ, a set of aptitudes and qualities for him to bring to fruition.

By the unaided effort of his own intelligence and his will, each man can grow in humanity, can enhance his personal worth, can become more a person.

But there is much more: by reason of his union with Christ, the source of life, man attains to new fulfillment of himself, to a transcendent humanism which gives him his greatest possible perfection: this is the highest goal of personal development.

Angels and Devils

In the beginning of time God created spiritual essences (angels) out of nothing.

The angels were subjected to a moral testing. Those angels who passed the test entered into the blessedness of heaven; those angels who did not pass the test were condemned to hell.

One task of the good angels is the protection of men and care for their salvation.

The devil possesses a certain dominion over mankind by reason of Adam's sin. From the very outset of his history man abused his liberty, at the urging of the Evil One.

Christ, True God and True Man

Among all the Scriptures, even those of the New Testament, the Gospels have a special preeminence, and rightly so, for they are the principal witness for the life and teaching of the incarnate Word, our Savior, about whom St. Paul says: "In times past, God spoke in fragmentary and varied ways to our fathers through the prophets; in this, the final age, he has spoken to us through his Son" (Hebrews 1:1).

The Son of God became man in order to redeem man from sin and reconcile him with God.

Christ was truly generated and born of a daughter of Adam, the Virgin Mary.

Christ assumed a real body, not an apparent body. He also assumed a rational soul.

Christ was free from all sin, from original sin as well as from all personal sin.

Christ is God.

He was sent by the Father to bring good news to the poor, to heal the contrite of heart, to seek and to save what was lost.

In His preaching Christ clearly taught the sons of God to treat one another as brothers.

Christ wrought miracles to illuminate His teaching and to establish its truth.

Wholly in accord with His mission, Christ remained, throughout His whole life, in a state of celibacy, which signified His total dedication to the service of God and men.

Christ underwent His passion and death freely, because of the sins of men and out of infinite love, in order that all may reach salvation.

He redeemed us from original sin and all the personal sins committed by each one of us. In Christ, God reconciled us to Himself and among ourselves.

On the third day after His death, Christ rose gloriously from the dead.

Christ gave His followers a new commandment to love one another, and promised the Spirit, their Advocate, who, as Lord and Life-giver, should remain with them forever.

Christ ascended body and soul into heaven and sits at the right hand of the Father.

He is now at work in the hearts of men through the energy of His Holy Spirit.

The four Gospels, whose historical character the Church unhesitatingly asserts, faithfully hand on what Jesus Christ, while living among men, really did and taught for their eternal salvation.

Christ's Mother and Ours

Mary most holy is the Mother of Christ, and consequently, the Mother of God and our spiritual Mother.

Mary was conceived without stain of original sin.

She conceived by the Holy Spirit without the cooperation of man. Mary bore her Son without any violation of her virginal integrity.

Also after the birth of Jesus, Mary remained a virgin.

Mary cooperated by her obedience, faith, hope and burning charity in the work of the Savior in giving back supernatural life to souls.

The whole life of the humble handmaid of the Lord was a life of loving service.

In Mary the Church finds the most authentic form of perfect imitation of Christ.

Mary was assumed body and soul into heaven.

Mary is Mother of the Church.

Mary shines forth to the whole community of the faithful as a model of the virtues.

Mary ever remains the path that leads to Christ.

Mary continues to fulfill from heaven her maternal function as the cooperator in the birth and development of divine life in the individual souls of redeemed men.

Christ's Church Continues His Mission

Before He was taken up into heaven, Christ founded His Church as the sacrament of salvation.

The Church is the Mystical Body of Christ; at the same time it is a visible society instituted with hierarchical organs, and a spiritual community.

The Church was founded for the purpose of spreading the kingdom of Christ throughout the earth for the glory of God the Father, and to enable all men to share in Christ's saving Redemption.

Christ, through the Apostles themselves, made their successors, the bishops, sharers in His consecration and mission.

Christ is the Head of the Church.

The Church is a sign to all in the world that Jesus Christ still stands in our midst.

Christ appointed the Apostle Peter to be the first of all the Apostles and to be the visible head of the whole Church.

According to Christ's ordinance, Peter is to have Successors in his primacy.

The Successors of Peter in the primacy are the Bishops of Rome. The Roman Pontiff, as the Successor of Peter, is the perpetual and visible source and foundation of the unity of the bishops and of the multitude of the faithful.

The Holy Spirit guides the Church into the fullness of truth and gives her a unity of fellowship and service. He furnishes and directs her with various gifts and adorns her with the fruits of His grace.

The Church speaks to man, more forcefully than anything else in his experience, concerning what he is, what he is for and why he yearns to attain something beyond, something outside himself.

The Church is that assembly which looks heavenward to pray "Abba, Father" and then earthward to greet all men as brothers. Thus, the Church is the keeper of each man as a brother because it is God's family.

Its law is the new commandment to love as Christ loves us.

The Sacraments—Actions of Christ

The sacraments are actions of Christ, which by the power of Christ impart grace.

All the sacraments of the New Covenant were instituted by Jesus Christ.

There are seven sacraments of the New Law: Baptism, Confirmation, Holy Eucharist, Penance, Anointing of the Sick, Holy Orders, and Matrimony.

Baptism confers the grace of justification—sanctifying grace.

Sanctifying grace makes the just man a friend of God, a child of God, and gives him a claim to the inheritance of heaven.

In Baptism the followers of Christ truly become sons of God and sharers in the divine nature. In this way they are really made holy.

They must hold on to and complete in their lives this holiness they have received.

By the Sacrament of **Confirmation,** the baptized are more perfectly bound to the Church, and the Holy Spirit endows them with special strength so that they are more strictly obliged to spread and defend the Faith, both by word and by deed, as true witnesses of Christ.

In the **Holy Eucharist,** Christ is present in a unique way, whole and entire, God and man.

Christ becomes present in the Sacrament of the Altar at the Consecration of the Mass by the transformation of the whole substance of the bread and wine into His Body and Blood. This mysterious change is called by the Church transubstantiation.

The Mass is the Sacrifice of Calvary rendered sacramentally present on our altars; it is a memorial of the death and resurrection of the Lord; it is a sacred banquet in which the People of God are nourished with the Body and Blood of the Lord.

After the Mass is celebrated, the Lord Jesus remains truly present in the Blessed Sacrament.

In the course of the day the faithful should not omit to visit the Blessed Sacrament, which is in the tabernacle, and which is the living heart of each of our churches. Such visits are a proof of gratitude, an expression of love, an acknowledgment of the Lord's Presence.

Especially from the Eucharist, as from a font, grace is poured forth upon us; and the sanctification of men in Christ and the glorification of God is achieved in the most efficacious possible way.

The grace by which we are justified may be lost, and is lost by every grievous sin. In the Sacrament of **Penance** we obtain pardon from the mercy of God for the offense committed against Him and are at the same time reconciled with the Church, which we have wounded by our sins. The Church's power to forgive sins extends to all sin without exception.

By the sacred **Anointing of the Sick** and the prayer of her priests, the whole Church commends the sick to the suffering and glorified Lord, asking that He may lighten their suffering and save them.

By the Sacrament of **Holy Orders** priests are consecrated to feed the faithful in Christ's name with the Word and the grace of God.

Matrimony and conjugal love are ordained for the procreation and education of children and for the mutual material and spiritual help of the spouses. As a mutual gift of two persons, this intimate union and the good of the children impose total fidelity on the spouses and argue for an unbreakable oneness between them.

Fortified by so many and such powerful sacraments, all the faithful, whatever their condition or state, are called by the Lord, each in his own way, to that perfect holiness whereby the Father Himself is perfect.

Eternity

The journey through this mortal life leads not only to the death of human flesh, but also to immortal life.

The souls of the just which in the moment of death are free from all guilt of sin and punishment for sin enter heaven.

The bliss of heaven lasts for all eternity.

The souls of the just which in the moment of death are burdened with venial sins or temporal punishment due to sins, enter purgatory.

The souls of those who die in the condition of personal grievous sin, enter hell.

The punishment of hell lasts for all eternity.

Before we reign with Him in glory, all of us will appear before Christ, our Judge, so that each one may receive what he has won through the body, according to his works, whether good or evil.

We look for the blessed hope and glorious coming of our God and Savior, Jesus Christ, who will refashion the body of our lowliness, conforming it to the body of His glory.

Appendix II

Guidelines for Christian Living

The Ten Commandments

1. I, the Lord, am your God. You shall not have other gods besides me.
2. You shall not take the name of the Lord, your God, in vain.
3. Remember to keep holy the Lord's day.
4. Honor your father and your mother.
5. You shall not kill.
6. You shall not commit adultery.
7. You shall not steal.
8. You shall not bear false witness against your neighbor.
9. You shall not covet your neighbor's wife.
10. You shall not covet anything that belongs to your neighbor.

The Eight Beatitudes

1. Blest are the poor in spirit; the reign of God is theirs.
2. Blest are the sorrowing; they shall be consoled.
3. Blest are the lowly; they shall inherit the land.
4. Blest are they who hunger and thirst for holiness; they shall have their fill.

5. Blest are they who show mercy; mercy shall be theirs.
6. Blest are the single-hearted; for they shall see God.
7. Blest are the peacemakers; they shall be called sons of God.
8. Blest are those persecuted for holiness' sake; the reign of God is theirs (Matthew 5:3-10).

Some Special Duties of Catholics

1. To keep holy the day of the Lord's resurrection: to worship God by participating in Mass every Sunday and holy day of obligation: to avoid those activities that would hinder renewal of soul and body.
2. To lead a sacramental life: to receive Holy Communion frequently and the Sacrament of Penance regularly:

    —minimally, to receive the Sacrament of Penance at least once a year (annual confession is obligatory only if serious sin is involved).

    —minimally, to receive Holy Communion at least once a year, between the First Sunday of Lent and Trinity Sunday. For a good reason, the precept may be fulfilled at another time during the year.
3. To study Catholic teaching in preparation for the Sacrament of Confirmation, to be confirmed, and then to continue to study and advance the cause of Christ.
4. To observe the marriage laws of the Church: to give religious training (by example and word) to one's children; to use parish schools and religious education programs.
5. To strengthen and support the Church: one's own parish community and parish priests; the worldwide Church and the Holy Father.

6. To do penance, including abstaining from meat and fasting from food on the appointed days.*
7. To join in the missionary spirit and apostolate of the Church.

Helpful Questions
for an Examination of Conscience

How much do I love God?

Do I love God and prove it by obeying His Ten Commandments?

Do I think about pleasing God, and try to live every day as well as I can?

Do I *believe* in God and trust Him? Or am I much more concerned about the things of this world?

Do I accept what the Catholic Church teaches?

Do I try to grow in knowledge and love of my Catholic Faith?

Am I courageous in professing my faith in God and the Church?

Am I proud to be a Catholic, willing to be known as one?

Do I say morning and evening prayers?

Do I turn to God often during the day, especially when I am tempted?

Do I love and reverence God's name? Have I taken His name in vain?

Have I blasphemed or sworn falsely?

Have I shown disrespect for our Lady and the saints?

Do I assist at Mass with attention and devotion on Sundays and holy days?

Have I fulfilled the precept of Communion during the Easter Time?

*Catholics are obliged to fast who have reached the age of eighteen but are not yet fifty-nine. Catholics fourteen years of age and over are obliged to keep the law of abstinence.

Are there "false gods" in my life: money, clothes, superstition, desire for popularity, that actually mean more to me than God does?

How much do I love my neighbor?

Do I really love my neighbor, or do I use people for my own ends? Do I do to them what I would *not* want done to myself?

Have I given bad example by my words or actions?

Do I contribute to the happiness of every member of my family?

Am I obedient and respectful to my parents?

If I am permitted, am I *willing* to share my possessions with those who have less, or do I look down on them?

Do I share in the apostolic and charitable works of the parish?

Do I pray for the needs of the Church and the world?

In school and at home, am I hardworking and conscientious in fulfilling my duties?

Am I truthful and fair? Did I ever damage another's good name?

Have I damaged another person's property or possessions? Have I stolen?

Have I quarreled? Made insulting remarks? Been angry?

Do I harbor hatred and a thirst for revenge?

How is my personal growth in the Christian life?

Do I think about heaven and hope for eternal life with God?

Do I pray often? Do I read God's Word, the Bible, and reflect on it?

Do I receive the Sacraments of Penance and Holy Eucharist regularly?

Am I pure in my thoughts, words, desires, actions?

Do I keep away from indecent literature, movies, dangerous companions, etc.?

Do I know how to make small acts of self-denial?

Do I really try to control my vices? To admit my mistakes? Or have I been proud, boastful, demanding on others?

Am I lazy? Do I waste a lot of time?

Do I use my talents and time to help others know Jesus?

Am I patient in accepting disappointments and sorrows?

INDEX

Daughters of St. Paul

MASSACHUSETTS
  50 St. Paul's Ave., Jamaica Plain, Boston, MA 02130; **617-522-8911.**
  172 Tremont Street, Boston, MA 02111; **617-426-5464; 617-426-4230.**
NEW YORK
  78 Fort Place, Staten Island, NY 10301; **212-447-5071; 212-447-5086.**
  59 East 43rd Street, New York, NY 10017; **212-986-7580.**
  625 East 187th Street, Bronx, NY 10458; **212-584-0440.**
  525 Main Street, Buffalo, NY 14203; **716-847-6044.**
NEW JERSEY
  Hudson Mall—Route 440 and Communipaw Ave.,
    Jersey City, NJ 07304; **201-433-7740.**
CONNECTICUT
  202 Fairfield Ave., Bridgeport, CT 06604; **203-335-9913.**
OHIO
  2105 Ontario Street (at Prospect Ave.), Cleveland, OH 44115;
    216-621-9427.
  616 Walnut Street, Cincinnati, OH 45202; **513-721-4838; 513-421-5733.**
PENNSYLVANIA
  1719 Chestnut Street, Philadelphia, PA 19103; **215-568-2638;**
    215-864-0991
VIRGINIA
  1025 King Street, Alexandria, VA 22314; **703-683-174ϊ; 703-549-3806.**
SOUTH CAROLINA
  243 King Street, Charleston, SC 29401.
FLORIDA
  2700 Biscayne Blvd., Miami, FL 33137; **305-573-1618; 305-573-1624.**
LOUISIANA
  4403 Veterans Memorial Blvd., Metairie, LA 70006; **504-887-7631;**
    504-887-0113.
  423 Main Street, Baton Rouge, LA 70802; **504-343-4057; 504-381-9485.**
MISSOURI
  1001 Pine Street (at North 10th), St. Louis, MO 63101; **314-621-0346;**
    314-231-1034.
ILLINOIS
  172 North Michigan Ave., Chicago, IL 60601; **312-346-4228; 312-346-3240.**
TEXAS
  114 Main Plaza, San Antonio, TX 78205; **512-224-8101; 512-224-0938.**
CALIFORNIA
  1570 Fifth Ave., San Diego, CA 92101; **619-232-1442.**
  46 Geary Street, San Francisco, CA 94108; **415-781-5180.**
WASHINGTON
  2301 Second Ave., Seattle, WA 98121; **206-623-1320; 206-623-2234.**
HAWAII
  1143 Bishop Street, Honolulu, HI 96813; **808-521-2731.**
ALASKA
  750 West 5th Ave., Anchorage, AK 99501; **907-272-8183.**

CANADA
  3022 Dufferin Street, Toronto 395, Ontario, Canada.